CW00539209

THE BEST OF THE GERS

THE RANGERS A-Z

Written by Graham Betts
Updated by Rob Mason

First published in the UK in 2007
Updated and reprinted in 2021

ISBN: 978-1782819363

Printed and bound printed in Europe

PICTURE CREDITS: Action Images, Alamy, Reuters, Getty Images, PA Photos, Wiki Commons.

CELEBRATIONS AFTER BEATING CELTIC 1-0 TO LIFT THE 1999 SCOTTISH FA CUP

ADVOCAAT

Born in the Hague on 27 September 1947, Dick Advocaat had a largely uneventful career as a player, but made his mark later as a coach, commencing at amateur side DVSP.

After two spells assisting the Dutch national team, he was appointed national coach in 1992 and guided the side to the World Cup finals in 1994, where they reached the quarter-finals before being beaten by Brazil.

Upon returning to Holland, Dick took over at PSV Eindhoven and enjoyed four success-laden years and ended Ajax's period of domination of the domestic game. In June 1998, he was appointed manager of Rangers, replacing Walter Smith.

Dick's appointment was seen by many as an attempt by Rangers to translate their domestic success into European competition, for despite having competed in the European Champions Cup for ten of the previous eleven campaigns, they had only once made any real impact. Dick's reputation as one of the Europe's top coaches was expected to change all of that.

A treble in his first season in charge proved that it was business as usual on the domestic front, even though Rangers slid out of the UEFA Cup in the third round. The following season saw Rangers clinch the double and, in their return to the European Champions League, record home and away victories over PSV Eindhoven, even though they were unable to progress beyond the group stage and went out of the UEFA Cup on penalties in the third round.

The 2000-01 season was a disappointing one that finished barren trophy-wise and Rangers fifteen points adrift of their greatest rivals Celtic at the top of the Premier League. After qualifying for the Champions League that season, Rangers made an impressive start, winning their opening two matches, but only two further points were secured and Rangers were eliminated, also losing their UEFA Cup tie with FC Kaiserslautern.

In December 2001, Dick Advocaat stepped down as manager of the club, to be replaced by Alex McLeish, but remained at Ibrox as director of football. Six months later, he left the club entirely and returned to Holland to take over as national coach for a second time, guiding them to the semi-finals of the 2004 European Championships. He later had a spell coaching at club level in Germany before returning to the international stage, taking over as South Korean coach and taking them to the 2006 World Cup finals.

From June 2006 to 2009 he successfully managed Zenit St. Petersburg taking them to the Russian Premier League title and also managing them against Rangers in the 2008 UEFA Cup final. After lifting that trophy, Advocaat's Russians then added the UEFA Super Cup by beating Manchester United.

He then managed the national sides of Belgium, Russia, Serbia and had a third spell in charge of the Netherlands. These moves into international football were interspersed with spells with AZ (twice), PSV again, Sunderland, Fenerbahce, Sparta Rotterdam, Utrecht and Feyenoord where he was still in charge at the age of 73 in 2021.

ALBERTZ SCORES AGAINST CELTIC AT IBROX, MARCH 2000

BELOW:
JORG CELEBRATES WINNING THE 2000 SCOTTISH CUP AFTER BEATING ABERDEEN 4-0

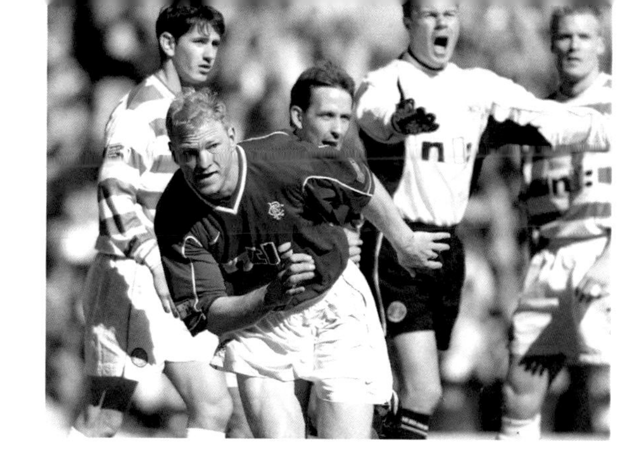

ALBERTZ

Born in Mönchengladbach on 29 January 1971, Jorg was a youth and apprentice player with PSV Mönchengladbach and Borussia Mönchengladbach before signing his first professional contract with Fortuna Dusseldorf in 1990.

Following the club's relegation to Division Two of the Bundesliga, Jorg was sold to SV Hamburg where he made his reputation, earning the nickname 'The Hammer' in recognition of his long-range shooting abilities and becoming club captain after two years.

In 1996, Walter Smith paid £4 million to bring the relatively unknown German to Ibrox Park, but he soon had the crowd on his side, especially after a stunning free-kick against Celtic in January 1997 that proved to be the catalyst to Rangers securing the League title for the ninth time in a row.

Whilst Jorg had been a virtual ever-present whilst Walter Smith was manager, the arrival of Dick Advocaat saw Jorg slip down the pecking order, and whilst he would ultimately collect medals for winning the championship in 1997, 1999 and 2000, it was plain that he was not part of Advocaat's long-term plans.

A £3.5 million fee took him back to SV Hamburg in 2001, having netted 82 goals for the Light Blues during his time with the club.

ATTENDANCES

Rangers' best attendances at Ibrox Stadium in each of the major competitions.

COMPETITION	OPPONENTS	DATE	ATTENDANCE
Scottish League	Celtic	01/01/1939	118,730
Scottish FA Cup	Hibernian	10/02/1951	102,342
Scottish League Cup	Celtic	16/10/1948	105,000
Europe	St Etienne	04/09/1957	85,000
	AC Milan	27/11/1957	85,000
	Leeds United	26/03/1968	85,000

JIM AND DENIS LAW PRACTICING BEFORE
SCOTLAND'S 1964 FIXTURE AGAINST IRELAND

BAXTER

Although Jim Baxter was a childhood Rangers fan, he began his career with Raith Rovers on a part-time basis whilst working as first a carpenter and then a collier. It was his abilities on the field, however, that attracted interest from bigger clubs, with Rangers enabling him to fulfil his childhood dream when they paid £17,500 in June 1960.

Jim was just 20 years of age at the time (he was born in Hill o' Beath in Fife on 29 September 1939) but marched straight into the first team, helping Rangers win the Scottish League and League Cup double at the end of his first season. There were to be a further two League titles, two League Cups and three victories in the Scottish FA Cup during the five years Jim was at Ibrox, a time when he was acknowledged as one of the most skilful players in the game. And yet the general consensus was that Jim's talent was largely allowed to go to waste, with his disinterest in training, tactics, discipline and just about everything else that goes to make a great player, all too often apparent.

On his day, on the field, he could be breathtaking, none more so than his performance in the darker blue shirt of Scotland in 1963 against England, when he inspired ten-man Scotland (his Rangers teammate Eric Caldow suffered a broken leg) to a 2-1 victory, scoring both goals, the first from the penalty spot with the first penalty he had ever taken in his life.

Unfortunately, most of his days off the field were spent drinking, womanising and gambling, with his condition suffering as a result. He was sold to Sunderland in 1965 as former Rangers stalwart and Scotland manager Ian McColl paid £72,500 for him. At Roker Park he dazzled with his skill, but disappointed with his application. Baxter believed in the ball doing the work, but not himself. Nottingham Forest then made him their first £100,000 player in December 1967, but he returned to Rangers in 1969, not even a shadow of his former self and retired from the game to become a publican.

JIM SENDS GORDON BANKS THE WRONG WAY FROM THE SPOT AT WEMBLEY 1963

Jim was later asked if the sums modern players were earning would have made any difference to his lifestyle, to which he replied 'Definitely. I'd have spent £50,000 a week at the bookies instead of £100'.

And yet Jim is still fondly remembered, both by those who follow Rangers, who claim he was the most skilful left-half the club ever had, and by those who follow the national side, who bombarded the poll organised by Radio Five Live with nominations to get the new Wembley footbridge named after him!

Jim Baxter, who won 34 caps for his country, died from cancer after a long battle on 14 April 2001.

BUTCHER

Born in Singapore on 28 December 1958, Terry was brought up in Suffolk and was spotted by Ipswich Town playing youth football in Lowestoft. Signed by the club in August 1976, he helped them win the UEFA Cup in 1981 and was first capped by England in 1980.

By 1986 he was widely regarded as the best centre-half in England and was the subject of intense transfer speculation, finally joining Graeme Souness' Ibrox revolution for £725,000 in August 1986.

Alongside fellow English recruits Chris Woods and Graham Roberts, Terry galvanised a Rangers side that had lived in their rival Celtic's shadow for too long, helping them win the Scottish League in 1987, 1989 and 1990 and the Scottish League Cup in three successive seasons, 1987, 1988 and 1989.

By the time of the 1990 World Cup, he was acknowledged as one of the best centre-backs in the world, a reputation he enhanced during the tournament, captaining the side to the semi finals in the enforced absence of Bryan Robson.

A few months later the end came to his Rangers career, Terry losing out after an argument with manager Graeme Souness and being sold to Coventry City in 1990 where he became player manager, as he later did at Sunderland before finishing his playing career with Clydebank.

As manager of Motherwell, his side gifted the 2004-05 League Championship to Rangers by beating Celtic on the final day. He went on to manage Sydney, Brentford, Inverness Caledonian Thistle, Hibernian, Newport County and finally the Philippines, having also had a caretaker spell at Partick Thistle.

BOYD

Released by Rangers as a boyhood full-back, Tarbolton-born Boyd cost the Gers half a million pounds on New Year's Day 2006, after making his name as a striker with Kilmarnock.

A debut hat-trick showed Kris intended to make up for lost time, and by the end of the season he was Rangers' top-scorer as well as Killie's, the first man to be top scorer at two clubs in the same season.

He went on to do the domestic cup double in 2007-08, the double of SPL and Scottish Cup the following season and SPL and League Cup a year later. For the first of those trophies, Kris contributed both goals in a 2-2 League Cup final draw with Dundee United before scoring the decisive spot-kick in the penalty shoot-out. He then scored two of the goals as Queen of the South were seen off 3-2 in the Scottish Cup final.

31 goals in 2008-09 saw him top-scorer as the league and cup were won and the following season he bagged five in a 7-1 demolition of Dundee United, before later that term adding another against the same team to register his 100th league goal for the Gers.

Top scorer again a year later as League and League Cup were won, Boyd went on to play in England, Turkey and the United States with Middlesbrough, Nottingham Forest, Eskisehirspor and Portland Timbers before coming back to Scotland, initially with Kilmarnock prior to returning to Rangers in the summer of 2014.

After a season at Ibrox, he moved back to Killie where in 2017-18, he was again top-scorer in the SPL. Boyd also scored seven times in winning 18 caps for Scotland.

CELEBRATIONS AFTER WINNING THE 2010 SCOTTISH PREMIER LEAGUE

CAIRNS

Born in Merryton on 30 October 1890, Tommy Cairns would go on to be a vital member of the Rangers side either side of the First World War, but for some reason only won six full caps for Scotland, a meagre figure given his worth to his club.

Tommy had begun his career in junior football with Burnbank Athletic and Larkhall Thistle before being lured south of the border to sign for Bristol City in 1911, but after only eleven appearances returned to Scotland to sign for Peebles Rovers.

He then had a brief spell with St Johnstone before finally being spotted by Rangers and joined the Ibrox outfit in November 1913, almost immediately ensconced as first choice inside-left, a position he was to hold for the next 13 years.

Tommy's time at Ibrox was rewarded with championship medals in 1918, 1920, 1921, 1923, 1924 and 1925, although he was unable to pick up a winners' medal

TOMMY WITH THE RANGERS TEAM, BACK ROW, THIRD FROM LEFT

in the Scottish Cup, having to settle for the runners-up variety in 1921 and 1922. All six of Tommy's international caps were awarded whilst he was associated with Rangers, the first coming in 1920, by which time he had formed an extremely effective left-wing partnership for both club and country with Alex Morton.Tommy remained at Ibrox until 1927, having made over 400 League appearances for the club, and returned to England to play for Bradford City, making 135 appearances for the Bantams before retiring in 1932. He later served Arsenal as their chief scout in Scotland before his death in 1967.

CALDOW

Born in Cumnock on 14 May 1934, Eric Caldow was fortunate enough to play in two great Rangers sides, at either end of his Ibrox career. Although Eric began his association with the club at the age of 14, he was sent out to Muirkirk Juniors in order to develop his talent and was eventually recalled to Ibrox at the age of 18.

The following season he made his debut in the League Cup win over Ayr United and would go on to make eight appearances for the club that term. In 1954-55, he made eleven League appearances and thereafter was a first-team regular, going on to collect championship medals in 1956, 1957, 1959, 1961 and 1963.

Initially used as a right-back, Eric was later successfully converted to left-back, but it did not matter where he played, his speed, both in thought and deed, were sufficient to enable him to get the better of almost any opponent. Eric was just as regular a player for Scotland, collecting his first cap in May 1957 against Spain and going on to collect 40, before a serious leg break brought his international career to an end. It almost did for his club career too, for Eric struggled back into the side and made just three appearances during the 1963-64 season. He recovered sufficiently to make 26 League appearances the following term, but it was in the League Cup that he enjoyed his finest moments that season, winning a third winners' medal in that competition to go with two in the Scottish Cup.

ERIC CALDOW AND JOHNNY HAYNES LEAD OUT THEIR TEAMS FOR THE 1961 ENGLAND V SCOTLAND CLASH AT WEMBLEY

After 407 appearances for Rangers he left at the end of the 1965-66 season spending a year with Stirling Albion before becoming player/manager of Corby Town and subsequently managing Stranraer from 1973 to 1975 after a spell in charge of Ayrshire Junior club Hurlford United. Eric was inducted into the Scottish Football Hall of Fame in 2007 and passed away at the age of 84 in March 2019.

A JUBILANT RANGERS TEAM LEAD BY ERIC CALDOW AFTER BEATING HEARTS 3-1 IN THE LEAGUE CUP FINAL

COOPER

Born in Hamilton on 25 February 1956, Davie began his professional career with Clydebank and proved an instant success, helping the club win successive promotions and a place in the Premier League by the end of the 1976-77 season.

His performances on the wing for Clydebank had not gone unnoticed by either the international selectors or scouts from bigger clubs, for he was drafted into the Scottish squad for the Home International Championships and summer tour of South America and became the subject of intense transfer speculation. It eventually cost Rangers £100,000 to secure his signature in June 1977, but it proved to be money well spent as Davie ended his first season at Ibrox having helped the club win the domestic treble.

Although Celtic finished the following term Champions, Rangers retained both cups, with Davie seemingly reserving his most effective performances for the cup campaigns.

Season 1979-80 saw Rangers finish empty-handed amid speculation that all was not well between manager John Greig and his star winger, with Davie's laid back attitude both on and off the pitch completely at odds with the style Greig had shown as a player. Brighton came in with an offer for both Davie and Gordon Smith, but Greig allowed only Smith to make the move south.

His Rangers career might have been saved, but it was not entirely resurrected, for Davie was in and out of the side during the 1980-81 season. His greatest performance came in the Scottish Cup final replay against Dundee United when he virtually tore United apart on his own.

Against the same opponents the following season, this time in the League Cup Final, Davie was again the difference between victory and defeat, proof that with him in the side, Rangers really were a force to be reckoned with.

After another barren season in 1982-83, John Greig made way for the returning Jock Wallace, the manager who had originally signed Davie and who played him more regularly, and whilst the League title proved elusive, there were still victories in the League Cup in 1984 and 1985 to savour.

Davie was to collect a further two League Cup winners' medals whilst with Rangers, in 1987 and 1988, scoring in both finals, by which time the manager at Ibrox had changed once again, with Graeme Souness taking the hot seat. He too began to use Davie sparingly and eventually he was transferred to Motherwell for £50,000 in August 1989. He had won three League titles, three Scottish Cups and seven League Cups whilst at Ibrox and still hadn't finished his trophy collection, adding a further Scottish Cup in 1991.

In December 1993 he returned to Clydebank, combining playing with coaching duties with the intention of retiring from playing at the end of the 1994-95 season in order to concentrate on coaching full time. Sadly, he was to suffer a brain haemorrhage whilst he and former Celtic player Charlie Nicholas were recording a coaching video for young people and died on 23 March 1995.

In the immediate aftermath of his death, supporters of virtually all clubs in Scotland lay scarves in homage to Davie at Ibrox, including more than a fair few of Celtic, recognition of his accomplishments in the dark blue jersey of Scotland (he won 22 caps) as well as the light blue of Rangers.

COOPER TAKES ON CELTIC'S MARK REID IN THE 1983 GLASGOW CUP FINAL

DAVIS

Born in Ballymena on New Year's Day 1985, midfield dynamo Davis went on to become Britain's most capped men's international when he won his 126th cap for Northern Ireland against Bulgaria in March 2021. In 2017, he received the MBE for Services to Football after captaining Northern Ireland at the 2016 European Championships.

Having started at Aston Villa, Davis made his senior debut in the Premier League against Norwich City. After over 100 appearances for Villa, Steve signed for his international manager Lawrie Sanchez at Fulham, but after just six months came to Rangers, initially on a six month loan.

Debuting against Panathinaikos in the UEFA Cup in February 2008 he went on to help Rangers reach the final in which he played against Zenit. He also won two winners medals that season, coming on as a sub as Queen of the South were beaten in the Scottish Cup final after he had scored in the penalty shoot-out when Dundee United were defeated in the League Cup show-piece. Steve completed a summer transfer from Fulham for a fee reported of £3m. Success continued to flow in his first full season when his Old Firm winner that took the Gers to the top of the table was the icing on the cake as Rangers won the SPL and retained the Scottish Cup. The following term saw Steve named PFA Players' Player of the Year as he helped regain the League Cup and retain the SPL.

In 2011, he scored in the final as Celtic were beaten in the League Cup and was hugely influential as the SPL was won again before he returned to England in 2012, moving to Southampton. He scored on his debut for the Saints against Manchester City and went on to play 226 times for the club before being drawn back to Ibrox in 2018 after seven seasons on the south coast of England.

Again the switch to Glasgow began with a loan, but blossomed once again as he helped guide Rangers to a 55th league championship in 2021.

DAWSON

One of the greatest goalkeepers the club ever signed, Jerry Dawson proved good enough to displace another Rangers legend in Tom Hamilton, and was virtually unrivalled as the number one at the club from 1933 to 1945 and went on to win 14 full caps for his country.

Born in Falkirk in 1909, Jerry joined Rangers in 1929 and made his debut in January 1931 against St Mirren and went on to collect five League championship and two Scottish Cup winners' medals. His tally in the latter might have been higher, for having helped Rangers reach the final in 1934, he was replaced by Tom Hamilton in the final against St Mirren.

Although proper League football was suspended for the duration of the Second World War, Jerry did help Rangers win two Scottish War Cups, two Summer War Cups and the Southern League Cup on one occasion. In 1944, he again helped Rangers to the final of the Southern League Cup, but suffered a broken leg in the match that saw Hibernian win 6-5 on corners.

Although the leg break was considered career threatening, he returned to the side in 1945 and went on to appear in the prestigious friendly against Dinamo Moscow. This proved to be virtually the end of his Rangers career, for he moved on to Falkirk soon after and spent four years at the club before retiring in 1949. He died on 19 January 1977.

RONALD DE BOER HOLDS UP THE 2003 LEAGUE TROPHY AFTER THE LEAGUE WIN AT DUNFERMLINE

DE BOER

Born in Hoorn, Holland on 15 May 1970, the twin brother of one-time fellow Rangers player Frank, Ronald played amateur football for De Zouaven and Lutjebroek before commencing his professional career with Ajax in 1988.

After three years with Ajax and never regarded as a regular, he switched to FC Twente and spent two years with the club, enhancing his reputation as a midfield player of considerable note. He returned to Ajax in 1992 and became a key component in the side that would win the UEFA Champions League in 1995.

A move to Barcelona followed in 1998, but he was used sparingly at the Nou Camp, prompting a £4.2 million swoop by Rangers in 2000, joining a growing number of Dutch internationals who could be found at Ibrox at the time. He helped the club win the domestic treble in 2002-03, scoring vital goals in all three competitions, including one in the final-day 6-1 League victory over Dunfermline that enabled Rangers to take the title on goal difference.

Injuries were to blight Ronald's 2003-04 season, which saw brother Frank also arrive at Ibrox, and at the end of the campaign, Ronald was told his contract would not be renewed.

He moved on to Qatar where he signed for Al-Rayyan for a season before having three years up to 2008 with Al-Shamal. He then stayed in Qatar as assistant coach to the country's Olympic and Under 23 team in 2010-11 before returning to Ajax to work in their youth system.

DRUMMOND

One of the first great full-backs the club ever had, Jock Drummond formed an extremely useful club partnership with Nicol Smith, immediately in front of the equally impressive goalkeeper Matt Dickie.

Jock was born in Alva in 1870 and began his career with Falkirk, earning the first of his 14 Scottish caps with the club before switching to Rangers in March 1892. He did not have to wait long before collecting his first honour, helping Rangers win the Scottish Cup in 1894 with victory over Celtic. There were further cup successes in 1897, 1898 and 1903, but it was the League that was the prime concern, and that took a little longer to arrive back at the club.

Although the trophy did arrive at Ibrox in 1899, Jock sat out most of the season owing to injury and so missed out on a medal, but more than adequate compensation was received when the League was retained in 1900, 1901 and 1902.

A no-nonsense defender, who favoured the immediate boot out of danger, rather than dwelling on the ball looking for a pass to a colleague, Jock was known for wearing a cloth cap whilst playing.

He ended his connection with Rangers in 1904 and returned to Falkirk to serve as a coach, later becoming a director of the club before his death in 1935.

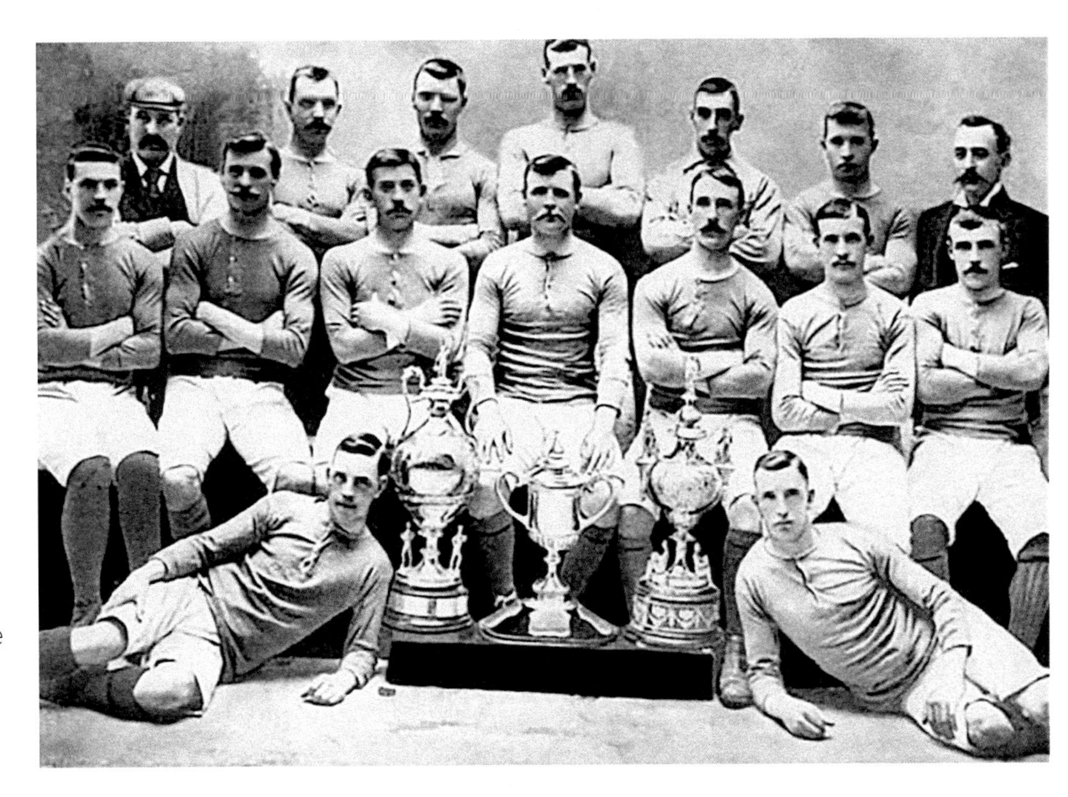

RANGERS 1896-97 SQUAD DRUMMOND PICTURED IN THE CENTRE

ENGLISH

Sam English scored a record 44 league goals in 1931-32. He was inducted into the Rangers Hall of Fame in 2009, and at this point, silversmith Cara Murphy was commissioned to produce a silver bowl containing 44 silver balls. Called The Sam English Bowl, this is presented annually to the club's top scorer, Kris Boyd being the first recipient.

Oddly, the season of Sam's sensational scoring was the only one in a nine-year sequence where the League title failed to come to Ibrox, although the Scottish Cup did, after English scored in the replayed final against Kilmarnock. Although English was a league champion a year later, an Irish international and listed Liverpool amongst his other clubs, he was forever dogged by being involved in the tragedy which resulted in the death of Celtic 'keeper John Thompson.

Absolved of any blame by an official enquiry, English was always linked to the incident by supporters up and down the country and suffered frequent references to the accident.

Thompson had dived at the feet of the onrushing English, blocked his shot, but then collided with Sam's knee. Rushed to the Victoria Infirmary, the stricken goalkeeper died that night despite surgery on the depressed fracture of his skull. Poor John Thomson was a Scotland international and only 22.

Sam English had been born in Crivolea in County Antrim on 18 August 1908. He joined Rangers in 1931, scored twice on his debut against Dundee and within a fortnight, netted five goals in a 7-3 victory over Morton. He had the superb record of 54 goals in his 60 league games for Rangers, but as well as enduring being remembered for the sad situation regarding John Thomson, he suffered from motor neurone disease and passed away in 1967 at the age of 58.

EUROPE

Looking ahead to a return to the Champions League in 2021-22, Rangers have a proud European Record. Winners of the European Cup Winners' Cup in 1971-72, the club were finalists in the same competition in 1966-67 and 1960-61, finalists in the UEFA Cup in 2007-08, contested the European Super Cup in 1972 and were European Cup semi-finalists in 1959-60.

Rangers first match in European competition was on 2 October 1956 as Nice were beaten 2-1 at Ibrox, Max Murray becoming the club's first European scorer. When being eliminated from the Europa League in the Round of 16 to Slavia Prague in April 2021 Rangers had the following European Record.

MAX MURRAY

	P	W	D	L	F	A
EUROPEAN CUP / CHAMPIONS LEAGUE	161	62	40	59	232	218
EUROPEAN CUP WINNERS' CUP	54	27	11	16	100	62
UEFA CUP/ EUROPA LEAGUE	122	56	37	29	182	120
UEFA SUPER CUP	2	0	0	2	3	6
INTER-CITIES FAIRS CUP	18	8	4	6	27	17
TOTAL	**357**	**153**	**92**	**112**	**544**	**423**

DAVID PROVAN JUBILANT
AFTER SECOND ROUND TRIUMPH
OVER BORUSSIA DORTMUND

EUROPEAN CUP WINNERS' CUP

Rangers' finest European moments, a few European Champions Cup/UEFA Champions League matches notwithstanding, have come in the now defunct European Cup Winners' Cup. Their first tilt at the competition came in the inaugural 1960-61 season when they reached the final, which was held over two legs for the first and only time in the competition's history.

Having overcome Wolverhampton Wanderers in the semi-final, Rangers were confident they could become the first British winners of a major European trophy, but particularly cynical opposition in the Italian club, Fiorentina won both legs to record a 4-1 aggregate victory, with Rangers also missing a penalty in the home leg.

Six years later, Rangers again made the final, disposing of West German holders Borussia Dortmund 2-1 on aggregate in the second round and winning the quarter-final against Real Zaragoza on the toss of a coin, with Rangers captain John Greig correctly calling after the two sides had finished level at 2-2 on aggregate.

Home and away victories over Slavia Sofia put Rangers into the final against the other West German entrants Bayern Munich, and with the final being held just down the road from Munich, in Nuremberg. Up against a side that could boast the talents of Sepp Maier, Franz Beckenbauer and Gerd Muller, Rangers could claim to have done well to contain their opponents to a single goal, scored eleven minutes into extra time, but Rangers' own deficiencies up front meant they lost 1-0.

Five years later, Rangers returned to the final, beating Bayern Munich in the semi-final, having lost to them in the Inter-Cities Fairs Cup the previous season.

Their opponents in the final were Dinamo Moscow, with the match being played at Barcelona's Nou Camp stadium. For fifty or so minutes, everything went Rangers' way, going into a 3-0 lead thanks to goals

WILLIE JOHNSTON SCORES HIS FIRST AND RANGERS' SECOND AGAINST MOSCOW DINAMO DURING THE 1972 FINAL

from Willie Johnston (two) and Colin Stein, although a late Russian rally brought the match back to 3-2 some three minutes from the end. Rangers held on to register their victory, with the thousands of Rangers fans in the stadium sweeping onto the pitch in celebration.

Whilst the relationship between the fans and the Spanish police had been cordial before and during the match, the police took the invasion to be something more sinister and responded by baton charging those on the field. The fans responded in kind and a battle royal ensued, with the result that the trophy and medal presentation was cancelled, with John Greig receiving the trophy in a small ante-room inside the stadium.

UEFA held Rangers responsible and banned the club from European competition for two years, later reduced to one on appeal, although Rangers did get to play Ajax in the two-legged European Super Cup, losing both legs in a 6-3 aggregate defeat.

BARRY CELEBRATES HIS GOAL IN RANGERS' 3-2 VICTORY OVER CELTIC IN THE 2002 SCOTTISH CUP FINAL

FERGUSON

The younger brother of former Rangers favourite Derek Ferguson, Barry was born in Glasgow on 2 February 1978 and was a schoolboy fan of the club, joining them as a junior at the age of 13 and being upgraded to the professional ranks in July 1994.

His first-team debut came in May 1997 after Rangers had tied up a ninth successive league title, but if was not until the appointment of Dick Advocaat that Barry became a regular. Indeed, Advocaat decided to build the side around Barry, with the Player being made club captain in October 2000 and helping them lift eight trophies over the next four years, including three League titles (1999, 2000 and 2003), two League Cups (2000 and 2003) and three Scottish Cups (2000, 2002 and 2003) as well as two domestic trebles and the accolade of Scottish Player of the Year in 2003.

Soon after the 2003-04 season kicked off, Barry was transferred to Blackburn Rovers for £7.5 million and the following year was appointed club captain in place of Garry Flitcroft by manager Graeme Souness.

Despite the responsibility of being captain, Barry never really settled at Blackburn and in January 2005 jumped at the chance of a return to Ibrox, costing Rangers £4.5 million and helping them win the League title with a last gasp win over Hibernian. He was awarded an MBE in the 2006 Queen's Birthday Honours List for his services to football.

He went on to help Rangers to the UEFA Cup final in 2008 before returning to England in 2009 playing for Birmingham City and Blackpool as well as having a loan with Fleetwood Town prior to becoming player/manager at Blackpool. From 2014 to 2017 he managed Clyde - playing once for them - before taking over at Kelty Hearts in 2018. Barry won 45 caps for Scotland.

FIFTY FIVE

Under Stevie G, Rangers strode to a record 55th league title in 2021, a record in any country. To 2020, Benfica had won 37 domestic league titles, Juventus 36, Real Madrid and Ajax 34, Bayern Munich 30, Barcelona 26, Manchester Utd 20, Liverpool 19, Milan and Inter 18, with Celtic on 51.

In France, no club has more than ten league titles. In Brazil, Palmeiras hold the record with 10, in Argentina, River Plate have 36, in Uruguay, Penarol have 50 and in Egypt, Al Alhy have been champions 42 times. So, wherever you look in the world, no club can match Rangers' Super 55.

The league title first resided at Ibrox in 1891 when in the first ever season of the Scottish League, the title was shared with Dumbarton after a Championship play-off finished all square at 2-2. As the century ended, Rangers took over. Champions in 1898-99, they won it for four seasons in a row at a time when no one had ever won it more than twice in succession. From 1910-11 to 1912-13, there was another three season dominance which was repeated from 1922-23 to 1924-25 having had three other titles in between. After one year without the title in 1925-26, the trophy was installed at Ibrox for a five-season sequence between 1926-27 and 1930-31.

JOE ARIBO LEADS THE CELEBRATION AFTER CALLUM McGREGOR'S OWN-GOAL SECURED A 1-0 WIN FOR RANGERS OVER CELTIC

After Motherwell pushed the Gers into second place in 1931-32, normal service was resumed with three more successive titles meaning that from 1923 until 1935, eleven out of 13 championships had come to the Light Blues. There were two more titles before World War two, at which point Rangers' 24 championships were five more than any other club.

Champions again in the opening post-war season, there would be another 13 titles before the next period of sustained dominance. Beginning in 1988-89 a superb nine-season run took the league title tally to 47. Relinquishing their grip on the trophy for a single season, the title immediately came back for the next two years. There were two more title wins before another three-year run from 2008-09 to 2010-11, before the glorious 55th title of a sensational 2020-21. It had been a long and winding road between numbers 54 and 55, but number 55 showed that without question, Rangers are now back on top.

FORMATION

Like many of today's famous football clubs, Rangers had a humble beginning, being little more than a boys' club when first formed in February 1872. According to legend, brothers Peter and Moses McNeil, William McBeath and Peter Campbell were walking through West End Park in Glasgow when they observed a group of men playing football and resolved to form their own side.

It was Moses who came up with the name Rangers, having spotted it in a book about rugby, and for the next few weeks the four set about training and recruiting others to join their team. By May of that year they had secured the services of Harry and William McNeil (Peter's and Moses's brothers), John Campbell (Peter's brother) John Hunter, Willie McKinnon and Willie Miller and others long since forgotten or never identified, and played their first match.

This was against Callender FC and was played at Flesher's Haugh on Glasgow Green, with the match ending as a bruising 0-0 draw.

Later that summer, Rangers played their second match, an 11-0 victory over Clyde (not the present Clyde side), although no record exists of the line-up and therefore the identity of who scored Rangers' first ever goal.

This is not entirely surprising, for who would have thought that what was then a youth side (no player was older than 20 years of age) would go on to become one of the most famous clubs in the world. What is known is that in this match the club wore the light blue shirt for the first time (in their opening match only four players had actually changed into something approaching a football kit, the rest playing in their street clothes), and even though today's shirt is nearer to royal blue in colour, the club are still known as the Light Blues.

By the spring of the following year, 1873, Rangers had recruited further players and held their first general meeting at which various club officers were elected. A year later, Rangers became members of the Scottish Football Association and entered into the Scottish FA Cup in October 1874. Nowadays a group of Rangers experts take a travelling Roadshow called 'The Founders' Trail' around the country telling the story of how Rangers came into being. The same enthusiasts also find abandoned graves of early Rangers greats and provide restoration work. Thefounderstrail.co.uk is the place to find out more about their work and Roadshow.

FORREST

Born in the Townhead area of Glasgow n 22 September 1944, Jim Forrest scored a phenomenal 57 goals in the 1964-65 season - a feat that remains a post-war British record.

This amazing total forms part of Forrest's overall tally of 145 in 163 games, which at the time made him Rangers' record post-war scorer - and his goals to games ratio remains the best since the war.

The first 50 of those goals arrived in just 45 appearances, while in 1965 and 1966 he bagged five goals in a game against Hamilton and later Stirling Albion. He also scored four goals in the 1963 League Cup final as Morton were mauled 5-0. A year later he only scored half as many in the League Cup final, but that was sufficient to see off Celtic 2-1.

Capped five times for Scotland, Forrest's fire was put out when he was discarded soon after being blamed by manager Scot Symon for the sensational 1967 Scottish Cup defeat to the Rangers of the Berwick variety.

Jim went on to play for Preston North End for a year prior to a five-year engagement with Aberdeen (62 goals in 192 games) where he won the Scottish Cup in 1970 before globe-trotting with stints at Cape Town City, Hong Kong Rangers and San Antonio Thunder, not forgetting a two-game loan with Hawick Royal Albert.

Perhaps the most amazing thing about Jim Forrest's fabulous goals record is that he was only 22 when Rangers let him go.

GAZZA CELEBRATES HIS GOAL
IN A 1995/96 PRE SEASON
FRIENDLY V STEAUA BUCHAREST

GASCOIGNE

Paul Gascoigne generated almost as many headlines for his off-the-field capers as he did for his on-the-field accomplishments, irrespective of where he happened to be playing. Born in Gateshead on 27 May 1967, he broke into the Newcastle United side whilst still a teenager and was proclaimed as one of the brightest midfield talents to have emerged in many a year, with none other than Jackie Milburn extolling his virtues.

He was sold to' Tottenham Hotspur for a then record £2 million in July 1988, subsequently breaking into the England first team and being one of the star performers in England's run to the World Cup semi-final in 1990.

The following season he was in inspirational form, scoring numerous vital goals, including a stunning free kick in the semi-final against Arsenal as Spurs made it to the FA Cup Final to face Nottingham Forest.

GASCOIGNE AFTER THE 4-3 VICTORY OVER HEARTS IN THE 1996 COCA-COLA CUP FINAL

RIGHT: GAZZA CELEBRATES SCORING AGAINST ABERDEEN, APRIL 96

Off the field there was mounting speculation that Paul might be sold to Lazio for some £8 million to alleviate growing debts, whilst on the field the player appeared to be hyped up for such a crucial match and was guilty of two sickening challenges. The second, on Gary Charles, resulted in Paul suffering serious cruciate damage and was put out of the game for over a year.

Paul did sign for Lazio for a reduced £5.5 million in May 1992 and spent just over three years in Italy before heading home in July 1995. He joined Rangers in a deal worth £4.3 million, seemingly still to fulfil the potential he had shown as a youngster.

Whilst he was to enjoy some success at Ibrox, helping the club win the League title in 1996 and 1997, the Scottish Cup in 1996 and the League Cup in 1997, the old demons were seldom far away.

An ill-advised decision to act as though playing the flute in a match against Celtic resulted in death threats from the IRA and he collected too many bookings for arguing with referees.

Some of the problems were not of his making, however, for in one match he found that referee Dougie Smith had dropped his yellow card and Paul retrieved it, brandishing it in front of the astonished referee as though to reprimand him for his carelessness. The less than amused referee failed to enter into the spirit of the occasion, booking Paul Gascoigne for his impertinence.

In March 1998, Paul was sold to Middlesbrough for £3.45 million, thus bringing to an end his at times turbulent Ibrox career, but he left friends and memories by the score.

GAZZA CELEBRATES THE SECOND OF HIS HAT-TRICK AGAINST ABERDEEN TO SEAL THE 1996 LEAGUE TITLE FOR RANGERS

GERRARD

Liverpool legend Steven Gerrard earned himself the same status at Rangers after leading his team to a spectacular league title in 2021. Having taken over at Ibrox in the summer of 2018, the man whose only previous managerial experience was with Liverpool's Under-18s and Under-19s showed he was ready for success on the big stage.

Runners-up in the league in his first two seasons when he took the Gers to the semi-final, then the final of the League Cup, along with the Europa League Round of 16 - featuring a fabulous win over Porto at a rocking Ibrox in the autumn of 2019 - he then brought the league title to the club for the 55th time and the first time in a decade. Stevie G had assembled an exciting attacking team that had blue flags flying in celebration all over the country.

One of the stand-out players of his generation, Stevie G was capped 114 times by England as well as captaining Liverpool with distinction.

A Champions League winner in 2005, he also won the UEFA Super Cup and UEFA Cup in 2001 as well as the League Cup three times, the FA Cup twice and the Community Shield.

A Merseysider born on 30 May 1980, on an individual level, Gerrard garnered a host of awards. These included the UEFA Club Footballer of the Year, the PFA Players' Player of the Year, the Football Writers' Footballer of the Year, being third in the Ballon d'Or Bronze Award as world player of the year, and being named in the English Premier League Team of the Year no fewer than eight times.

GOLDSON

Born in Wolverhampton on 18 December 1992, 6' 3" centre-back Connor Goldson played over 100 games for his first club Shrewsbury Town, had a spell on loan to Cheltenham Town and played 32 league games for Brighton & Hove Albion before crossing the border to come to Glasgow in June 2018.

Debuting against FK Shkupi of Macedonia in a Europa League qualifying game, he wore the captain's armband against St. Mirren within a couple of months of joining the club and celebrated with his first goal in a 2-0 win.

Goals have become a feature of the defender's colossal contribution. This was never better seen than when he bagged both in a 2-0 win away to Celtic in October 2020, but he also developed a pleasing penchant for goals in European competition, including one in a narrow win over Standard Liege at Ibrox a couple of months after his heroics at Celtic Park. A rock at the heart of defence as the Scottish Premiership was won in 2021, Connor was pure gold.

GOLDSON SCORES AGAINST CELTIC AT IBROX, OCTOBER 2020

LEFT:
GOLDSON CELEBRATES VICTORY OVER CELTIC AT CELTIC PARK, DECEMBER 2019

GORAM

Born in Bury on 13 April 1964, goalkeeper Andy Goram began his playing career with Oldham Athletic and spent seven seasons at Boundary Park, winning the first four of his 43 caps for Scotland whilst with the club. He joined Hibernian in 1987, but was unable to lift the Edinburgh club above mid-table mediocrity, although he continued to add to his tally of international caps.

A £1 million fee took him to Rangers in June 1991 and he stepped straight into the first team, helping them win the League title six seasons in succession and thus complete the infamous 'nine in a row' as well as two Scottish Cups and two League Cups. Andy was one of the star performers during Rangers' European exploits in 1992-93, which saw them come within one match of reaching the final of the UEFA Champions League.

When his Rangers career came to an end, he played for Motherwell, Notts County, Sheffield United, Manchester United, Coventry City, Queen of the South and Elgin City before turning to coaching, currently serving Airdrie United as goalkeeping coach.

Andy was an often controversial figure owing to his supposed political allegiances and when he was diagnosed as schizophrenic, opposing fans cruelly took delight in chanting 'Two Andy Gorams, There's Only Two Andy Gorams'!

Andy was also a talented cricketer, appearing for the Scottish cricket side four times, twice against Ireland and twice in the Nat West Trophy, bowling out England Test player Richard Blakey in a NatWest Trophy match against Yorkshire in 1989.

GOUGH

RICHARD CELEBRATES WITH THE 1993 CHAMPIONSHIP TROPHY

Born in Stockholm to a Swedish mother and Scottish father on 5 April 1962, Richard Gough grew up in South Africa and came to Scotland in 1980 to play in a trial for Rangers. They turned him down after which he joined Dundee United.

Although Richard briefly returned to South Africa suffering from homesickness, he eventually returned to Dundee United helping them win the Scottish League in 1983. Richard was to spend six seasons with Dundee United and by 1986, a number of bigger clubs were clamouring for his signature.

Although Rangers were believed to have offered £900,000 for him, Dundee United apparently would not sell him to another Scottish club and so he went to Spurs for £750,000. He was to spend a little over a year there, helping Tottenham reach the FA Cup Final in 1987, but by December 1987, Rangers got their man, Graeme Souness paying £1.1 million. Made captain he would go on to lead the club to the nine consecutive League titles, forming a particularly effective club partnership with Terry Butcher.

Richard remained at Ibrox until 1997 when he joined Kansas City Wizards in the United States Major League, subsequently going on to play for San Jose Clash. Richard's playing career came to an end with spells at Everton (where he was reunited with former Rangers manager Walter Smith) and Nottingham Forest and he eventually returned to Scotland in November 2004 to take over as manager of Livingston.

Although he saved the club from relegation from the Premier League, he resigned in May 2005 and returned to America for family reasons. Qualified to play for Sweden, South Africa or Scotland he chose Scotland and won 61 caps.

GREATEST XI

Do you agree with this Greatest Gers XI?

1 Allan McGregor
2 John Greig
3 Sandy Jardine
4 Richard Gough
5 Terry Butcher
6 Jim Baxter
7 Davie Cooper
8 Paul Gascoigne
9 Ally McCoist
10 Alfredo Morelos
11 Brian Laudrup

11
6
9
8
10
7

JOHN GREIG TUSSLES WITH CELTIC'S HARRY HOOD

GREIG

One of the finest servants the club has ever had, John Greig was born in Edinburgh on 11 September 1942 and grew up a Heart of Midlothian fan. Despite this, he has served only one club throughout his career, Rangers, and is regarded by many both inside and outside the club as the Greatest Ever Ranger, an accolade he was awarded after a 1999 vote among supporters.

He scored on what was his first team debut, against Airdrie in a League Cup match in 1961 and would go on to register 857 appearances for the first team, including 498 in League matches alone.

His time as a player saw him collect five League titles, six Scottish Cups and four League Cups, figures that include three domestic doubles, in 1964, 1976 and 1978. Perhaps his finest moment came in 1972, when he collected the European Cup Winners' Cup, although the event was overshadowed by rioting on the pitch by Rangers supporters and the cup was actually collected out of sight in the dressing room after the match.

Whilst his worth to Rangers was never questioned, he was equally vital to the Scottish national side, winning 44 caps for his country between 1964 and 1971 and captaining the side for three years. At the end of his playing career, which saw him named Player of the Year twice, he was awarded a testimonial by Rangers that drew a crowd of 65,000 for a match against Scotland at Ibrox, with John scoring twice in the 5-0 win.

Following his retirement he turned to management, taking over from Jock Wallace and bringing further Scottish Cup and League Cup success, although the League title itself proved elusive.

Although his time as manager was not as successful as many had hoped, he was responsible for bringing in many great Rangers players, including Ally McCoist, Derek Ferguson and Robert Fleck.

He resigned in 1983 to be replaced by the returning Jock Wallace, going into broadcasting and travel management but still a regular sight around Ibrox. In January 1990 he returned to Rangers on a more permanent basis, being appointed director of public relations. Appointed as a director in 2004 he resigned in October 2011 after the club was taken over. He returned in May 2015 becoming the club's honorary life president.

JOHN GREIG, VOTED THE CLUB'S GREATEST EVER RANGER

LEFT: **JOHN GREIG STATUE OUTSIDE IBROX**

MARK CELEBRATES HIS WINNING GOAL
IN THE 3-2 WIN OVER ABERDEEN IN 1995

HATELEY

The son of former footballer Tony Hateley (Chelsea, Liverpool and Villa, among others), Mark was born in Liverpool on 7 November 1961 and began his professional career with Coventry City, another of his father's former clubs, and would go on to make more than 100 appearances for the Sky Blues. While with Coventry he spent the summer of 1980 playing for Detroit Express in the USA.

He joined Portsmouth for £220,000 in 1983 and made an immediate impact, scoring 22 League goals in just 32 appearances and was rewarded with his first cap for England. Whilst many of England's bigger sides cast envious eyes at Mark, it was AC Milan of Italy that stepped in with a £915,000 offer in 1984.

Nicknamed Attila by the AC Milan fans, he proved immensely popular and effective and would spend four years with the club. He then joined AS Monaco and helped them win the French League title before a further £1 million move to Rangers in the summer of 1990. Whilst he had enjoyed considerable success prior to his move to Ibrox, it was his time at Rangers that proved most rewarding.

Five League titles, two Scottish Cups and three League Cups tell the story in bare statistics, but Mark's exploits in the Light Blue shirt were more the stuff of 'Roy of the Rovers' - his two goals against Aberdeen in the final match of the 1990-91 season snatched the title away from their opponents in dramatic fashion.

In November 1995, he joined the other Rangers, Queens Park Rangers of London in a £1.5 million deal but struggled to win over the fans, prompting a loan move to Leeds United. They knew all about his abilities, having been on the receiving end of a thunderbolt goal in the European Champions League in 1991.

MARK'S LATE LEVELLER IN THE 2-2 EUROPEAN CUP ENCOUNTER WITH MARSEILLE AT IBROX 1992

In March 1997, Mark sensationally returned to Ibrox to help out a side decimated by injury and helped them win the title again, the key result being a 1-0 win over Celtic that saw Mark sent off, but do enough whilst on the field to put Celtic off their stride.

The three wins Rangers recorded with Mark in the side that season enabled them to finish five points ahead of Celtic at the end of the campaign.

Released on a free transfer, Mark then took over as player-manager of Hull City before briefly coming back to Scotland to play two games for Ross County. In total Hateley scored a tremendous 229 goals in 619 club games across five countries in addition to nine goals in 32 games for England. His son Tom carries on the family trade by playing in England, Scotland with Dundee and in 2021 in Poland with Piast Gliwice.

LEE WALLACE HOISTS ALOFT THE
2016 SCOTTISH CHAMPIONSHIP TROPHY

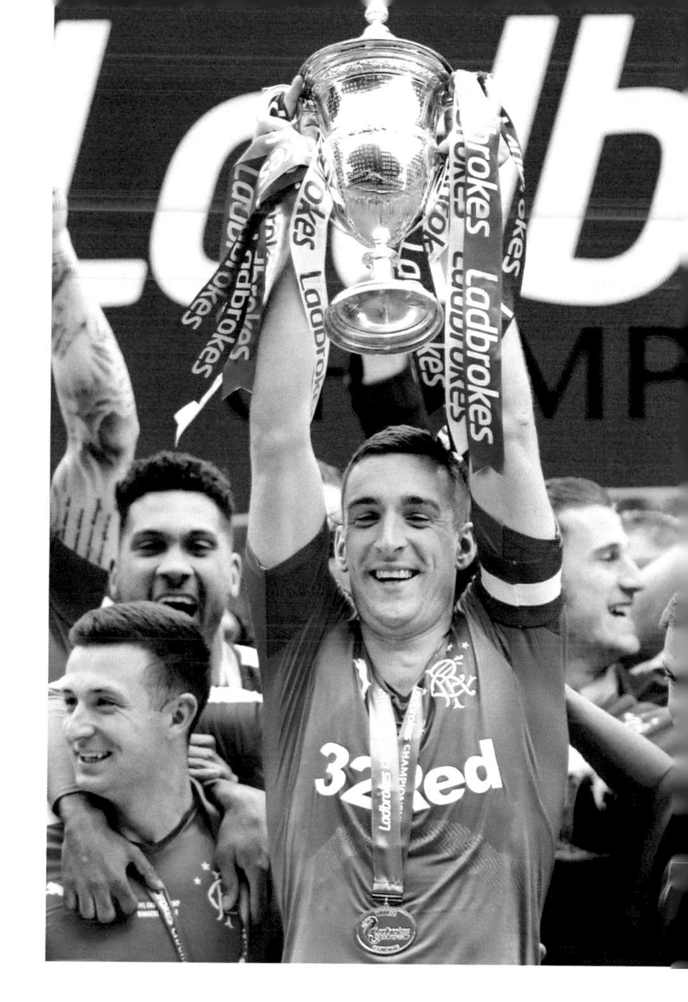

HONOURS

Scottish League Champions

1891 * 1899 1900 1901 1902 1911 1912
1913 1918 1920 1921 1923 1924 1925
1927 1928 1929 1930 1931 1933 1934
1935 1937 1939 1947 1949 1950 1953
1956 1957 1959 1961 1963 1964 1975
1976 1978 1987 1989 1990 1991 1992
1993 1994 1995 1996 1997 1999 2000
2003 2005 2009 2010 2011 2021

*Joint champions

Scottish Second Tier League Championship

2016

Scottish Third Tier League Championship

2014

Scottish Fourth Tier League Championship

2013

Scottish FA Cup winners

1894 1897 898 1903 1928 1930 1932
1934 1935 1936 1948 1949 1950 1953
1960 1962 1963 1964 1966 1973 1976
1978 1979 1981 1992 1993 1996 1999
2000 2002 2003 2008 2009

Scottish League Cup winners

1946 1948 1960 1961 1963 1964 1970
1975 1977 1978 1981 1983 1984 1986
1987 1988 1990 1992 1993 1996 1998
2002 2003 2005 2008 2010 2011

SCOTTISH PREMIER LEAGUE CHAMPIONS 2005

European Cup Winners, Cup winners

1972

Glasgow Cup

1893 1894 1897 1898 1900 1901 1902
1911 1912 1913 1914 1918 1919 1922
1923 1924 1925 1930 1932 1933 1934
1936 1937 1938 1940 1942 1943 1944
1945 1948 1950 1954 1957 1958 1960
1969 1971 1975* 1976 1979 1983 1985
1986 1987

*Trophy shared

Glasgow Merchants and Charity Cup

1879 1897 1900 1904 1906 1907 1909
1911 1919 1922 1923 1925 1928 1929
1930 1931 1932 1933 1934 1939 1940
1941 1942 1944 1945 1946 1947 1948
1951 1955 1957 1960

Scottish Challenge Cup

2016

IBROX

The Boys' club that the McNeil brothers Peter and Moses helped form in 1872 played their first matches on Glasgow Green, with Peter McNeil often having to arrive at the chosen venue extremely early in order to ensure the pitch was marked and ready and, more importantly, not taken by another team.

Such was the way of football in the nineteenth century, with the arrangement of a fixture no guarantee that the match would take place, especially if another club, with bigger and older boys, had taken a shine to the carefully marked pitch.It was Queen's Park's refusal to meet Rangers in a friendly as they had no pitch of their own that prompted the decision to search for their own enclosure. The first of these was found at Burnbank in 1875, near Kelvin Bridge, a ground that was sufficiently close to where many of the then players lived, and was formally opened with a fixture against Vale of Leven, then probably the second most famous club in the land, with Rangers drawing the historic fixture 1-1 on 11 September 1875.

Less than a year later, in August 1876, Rangers left Burnbank for Kinning Park, a ground that had previously been home to Clydesdale (the previous occupants moved to Titwood) and a month later Vale of Leven again provided the opposition, winning 2-1 on 2 September 1876.

Kinning Park was to remain Rangers' ground for the next ten years, increasing the capacity from 2,000 (a crowd of 1,500 witnessed the opening match against Vale of Leven) to 7,000 and making numerous improvements to both the pitch and facilities for spectators, although this ground was leased and by 1884 there came rumours that the landlords would eventually like the site back for other development. In the event, Rangers held on to it until February 1887, finishing the season at Cathkin Park, but having already secured another property a few miles west of Kinning Park.

RANGERS LEGENDS V AC MILAN GLORIE, MARCH 2012

The pitch was surrounded by a running track, with a grandstand capable of seating 1,200 built along one side, and a pavilion, with changing rooms, bathrooms and offices, was constructed in one corner. The first Ibrox Park was officially opened with a friendly match against Preston North End on 20 August 1887, with the 'Invincibles' winning 8-1 when the match was abandoned after some 70 minutes when the crowd, which some numbered some 15,000, spilled out onto the field.

VICTIMS ARE STRETCHERED AWAY AFTER A SECTION OF THE IBROX TERRACING COLLAPSED, 1902

Rangers outgrew this home too and so began work on an adjacent site on an even grander scale. A two-storey pavilion was built in the south-east corner, together with a grandstand, with the roof taken from the previous Ibrox ground, provided seating and cover for 4,500.

The new Ibrox Park comprised some 14.5 acres of land and could, claimed the club, hold 80,000 spectators, although 75,000 would be nearer the mark. It was this capacity figure that led to Ibrox being chosen to host the Scotland and England fixture in April 1902, but a significant part of the crowd was to be accommodated on wooden terracing, which in turn was on an iron framework, hardly the safest of environments.

So it proved, for midway through the match, seven rows of terracing just simply collapsed, sending hundreds down into the void that had been created. Twenty-five died and a further 587 were injured, many seriously. The wooden terracing was subsequently removed, reducing Ibrox's capacity to 25,000 in 1905.

Extensive work done by Archibald Leitch, the pre-eminent football ground designer, saw the construction of a massive grandstand, which would seat 10,500 and hold thousands more standing in the enclosure, the undoubted focal point of a ground that was elliptical in shape. Ibrox's capacity grew and grew, from 60,000 in 1905 to 80,000 after the First World War and beyond 100,000 by the time of the Second World War, with more than 118,000 packing in for the fixture against Celtic on 1 January 1939.

GATES TO IBROX STADIUM AT BROOMLOAN STAND

Although much work went into getting as many spectators into the ground as was possible, little or no thought appeared to be given to how they would leave the ground after matches.

Fans turn up for matches over a number of hours, but try to leave in a matter of minutes as soon as the game is over, a major factor in the events of another New Year's clash with Celtic, this one in 1971.

Stairway 13 had proved a hazard for much of the stadium's history, with numerous incidents prior to 1971, but it was this 1-1 draw that was to see one of the worst disasters in British sporting history, with 66 spectators dead from traumatic asphyxiation after someone was believed to have tripped over at the top of the stairway.

Over the next ten years, Ibrox changed out of all recognition, with the elliptical shape disappearing and a rectangular ground arising in its place. The Archibald Leitch stand remains, an almost constant reminder of Ibrox's former glories, but three brand new stands, almost identical in design and construction, gave the ground a capacity of just over 46,000.

Later work in filling in the corners, creating an enclosed stadium with a capacity of 50,817, turned Ibrox into one of the most impressive stadiums in the world.

JARDINE

Born in Edinburgh as William Pullar Jardine on 31 December 1948, Sandy was a childhood Hearts fan but joined Rangers as a youngster, making his debut for the club as an 18-year-old against Hearts in 1967, with Rangers running out 5-1 winners in the match at Ibrox.

Sandy would go on to make 674 appearances for Rangers, most of them as a full-back, although he was occasionally switched to sweeper, and was even used as an emergency striker for a spell, such was his devotion to the Rangers cause.

Above all else he was a fair player, earning admiration from both colleagues and foes alike for his belief in playing the game the right way. This style brought its own rewards, for Sandy was to win the Player of the Year award twice alongside numerous domestic honours with Rangers, as well as being an integral part of the side that won the European Cup Winners' Cup in 1972.

Capped 34 times by Scotland, he formed a particularly effective international partnership with Celtic's Danny McGrain and played in both the 1974 and 1978 World Cup campaigns. He was released by Rangers in 1982 and joined his boyhood team Hearts, going on to amass more than 1,000 appearances for his two clubs.

He subsequently became assistant manager and then joint-manager at Tynecastle before leaving the game altogether to pursue a career in business in 1988. Sandy later returned to Ibrox to work for the commercial department.

Sandy passed away in April 2014 after contracting liver cancer. In his honour, later the same year, the name of the Govan Stand was changed to the Sandy Jardine Stand.

JOHNSTON

Born in Glasgow on 30 April 1963, Maurice Johnston is one of only a handful of players to have played for both Rangers and Celtic, although none of the previous players attracted quite as much attention as Mo subsequently did. He had begun his career with Partick Thistle in 1981 and scored 41 goals during his two and a half seasons with the club, prompting a raid by Watford that saw Mo appear in the FA Cup Final in 1984.

After a season and a half south of the border, Mo returned north to sign for Celtic, the club he supported as a boy, and scored 71 goals during his three years at Parkhead. In 1987 he left for France and Nantes on a two-year contract, announcing initially that he had no intention of ever returning to Scotland. During his two years he had a change of mind, subsequently announcing at a press conference that he would return to Celtic once his contract ran out.

When he was finally unveiled in Glasgow in July 1989, however, it was as a Rangers player! Celtic fans branded him a traitor, whilst the transfer was hardly universally greeted at Ibrox, with some fans demonstrating outside the stadium and burning their scarves and season tickets as Rangers knowingly signed a Catholic for the first time.

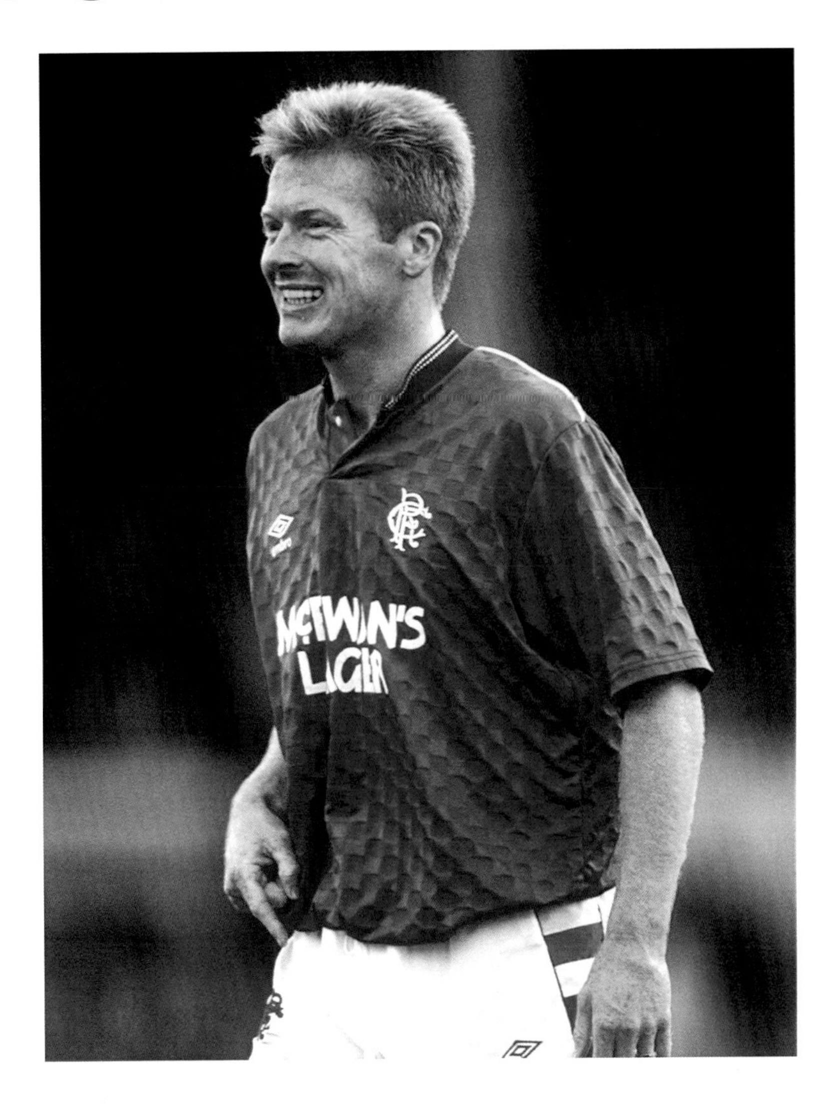

MO CELEBRATES RANGERS' LEAGUE TITLE SUCCESS OF 1991

Even Mo Johnston acknowledged the situation he now found himself in, claiming that he had managed to unite Glasgow, for now both Rangers and Celtic fans hated him! To further add to his woes, UEFA fined him £3,500 for 'unsporting conduct' for reneging on his return to Celtic Park!

A tally of 51 goals in 110 appearances for Rangers no doubt went some way to placate the Rangers faction that had been most vociferous against his arrival (though quite what it did for Celtic fans has never been revealed) and perhaps paved the way for other Catholics who have since signed for the club.

Mo remained at Ibrox until 1991 when he left to join Everton in a £1.5 million deal. He later returned to Scotland, with significantly less fanfare, to play for Hearts and Falkirk.

He finished his playing career in America with Kansas City Wizards and later became coach and then manager to the MetroStars, a team that later became re-branded as Red Bull New York. He also managed Toronto FC.

DEREK PLAYING FOR RANGERS
V DUNDEE UNITED 1979

JOHNSTONE

Born in Dundee on 4 November 1953, Derek Johnstone was a schoolboy fan of Dundee United and trained with the club as a youngster, but subsequently joined Rangers as a schoolboy in December 1968, being upgraded to the professional ranks in July 1970.

That same year he ensured his place in the record books, earning a place in the League Cup Final side to face Celtic whilst still ten days short of his seventeenth birthday and headed home the only goal of the game to secure the trophy. That was to be the first of many he won whilst with the club, collecting a total of three League titles, the Scottish Cup five times and the League Cup five times as well as a winners' medal from the European Cup Winners' Cup in 1972.

Whilst he favoured playing at centre-half, such was his versatility he also slotted in at centre-forward and in the midfield, performing in all three areas for both club and country and going on to win 14 caps for Scotland.

DEREK JOHNSTONE IN THE SCOTLAND WORLD UP SQUAD, ARGENTINA 1978

Derek remained at Ibrox until 1983 when he was sold to Chelsea for £30,000, but struggled to command a regular place in the side, prompting a loan move to Dundee United and then an eventual return to Ibrox.

His second stint at the club was not as successful as his first and he left the club for good in 1986 and after a brief spell as player-manager of Partick Thistle left the game in order to pursue a media career which has included working for Rangers TV.

In all, Derek hit 209 goals in 547 first-team appearances for Rangers, one of the best post-war records.

KLOS

Born in Dortmund on 16 August 1971, Stefan Klos began his professional career with his local side Borussia Dortmund in 1991, going on to help them win the UEFA Champions League in 1997 with a 3-1 win over Juventus. Despite this victory, Stefan was soon at odds with the German club over his contract and was eventually allowed to leave in December 1998, joining Rangers for £700,000.

He soon proved the ideal long-term replacement for Andy Goram, helping the club win the League and Scottish Cup at the end of the season. He has since gone on to add a further three League titles, three Scottish Cups and two League Cups, proving to be a resounding success as the last line of defence. Although overlooked at international level, his worth to Rangers has always been appreciated, being appointed captain in the summer of 2004.

Despite suffering a cruciate ligament injury in 2005 Stefan went on to play 298 games in all competitions before his retirement. He was inducted into the Rangers Hall of Fame in 2009.

KING

Dave King never played a game, but played a significant role in helping Rangers recover from their darkest hour. Glasgow-born, employment took him to South Africa where he earned his fortune. In March 2000, he became a non-executive director of Rangers and was reported to have invested £20m into Murray Sports Ltd.

Following the club going into administration on Valentine's Day 2012, King's love for Rangers saw him strive to bring the club out of administration. Despite that attempt being unsuccessful as Rangers FC entered liquidation at the beginning of 2015, he acquired almost 15% of the shares in Rangers International Football Club, the owners of Rangers FC. This made him the largest sole shareholder of the club of which he later became chairman between May 2015 and March 2020, when he was succeeded by Douglas Park.

Now resident in South Africa, Dave King celebrated Rangers' 2021 title with a £3,500 bottle of Yquem 1872 sweet wine, a bottle from the year the club were founded. Many a Rangers fan would join in with a toast to him.

LAUDRUP

The younger brother of the equally famous Michael Laudrup, Brian was born in Vienna, Austria on 22 February 1969, the son of former Danish international Finn Laudrup. Brian began his playing career with Brondby and earned his first international cap aged just 18 in the 1-0 defeat by West Germany in November 1987.

He became a regular in the Denmark side in 1989 and earned a big money move to Uerdingen for £650,000 having been named Danish Player of the Year. The following season he was sold to Bayern Munich for £2million and would go on to enhance his reputation, helping Denmark win the 1992 European Championships after they were drafted in as late replacements for Yugoslavia.

Brian then had a spell in Italy with Fiorentina and then AC Milan on loan, but his time in Italy was not a success, also hindering his international career as Denmark failed to qualify for the 1994 World Cup. In July 1994 he was sold to Rangers for £2.3 million and set about restoring his reputation as one of the most exciting players in the game, able to both create and finish chances with equal aplomb.

LAUDRUP CELEBRATES SCORING THE ONLY GOAL OF THE GAME AT CELTIC, 14/11/1996

His time at Ibrox brought success in the form of three League titles, the Scottish Cup and three League Cup victories, although by 1997 he was the subject of several bids from other clubs, with Ajax believed to have made a £5 million offer for his signature.

Brian decided to sit tight and see out his contract, which had another year to run and then move on, eventually joining Chelsea. Expectation was not matched by accomplishment however, and he moved on to FC Copenhagen and then Ajax before injury forced him to retire at the age of 31.

LAUDRUP GETS AWAY FROM CELTIC'S PHIL O'DONNELL DURING THE 1998 SCOTTISH CUP SEMI FINAL 2-1 VICTORY

In total he scored 21 times in 82 games for his country, was Danish Footballer of the Year four times and in 1992 was listed as the fifth best player in the world by FIFA.

After retiring he became a commentator for the UEFA Champions League for Danish TV as well as setting up a youth football camp with former Danish goalkeeper Lars Hogh and playing for Old Boys side Lyngby Boldklub.

LEAGUE POSITIONS

SEASON ENDING	POS	P	W	D	L	F	A	Pts
1891	Joint 1st	18	13	3	2	58	25	29
1892	5th	22	11	2	9	59	46	24
1893	2nd	18	12	4	2	41	27	28
1894	4th	18	8	4	6	44	30	20
1895	3rd	18	10	2	6	41	26	22
1896	2nd	18	11	4	3	57	39	26
1897	3rd	18	11	3	4	66	30	25
1898	2nd	18	13	3	2	71	15	29
1899	1st	18	18	0	0	79	18	36
1900	1st	18	15	2	1	69	27	32
1901	1st	20	17	1	2	60	25	35
1902	1st	18	13	2	3	43	29	28
1903	3rd	22	12	5	5	56	30	29
1904	4th	26	16	6	4	80	33	38
1905	2nd	26	19	3	4	83	28	41
1906	4th	30	15	7	8	58	48	37
1907	3rd	34	19	7	8	69	33	45
1908	3rd	34	21	8	5	74	40	50

SEASON ENDING	POS	P	W	D	L	F	A	Pts
1909	4th	34	19	7	8	91	38	45
1910	3rd	34	20	6	8	70	35	46
1911	1st	34	23	6	5	90	27	52
1912	1st	34	24	3	7	86	34	51
1913	1st	34	24	5	5	76	41	53
1914	2nd	38	27	5	6	79	31	59
1915	3rd	38	23	4	11	74	47	50
1916	2nd	38	25	6	7	87	39	56
1917	3rd	38	24	5	9	68	32	53
1918	1st	34	25	6	3	66	24	56
1919	2nd	34	26	5	3	86	16	57
1920	1st	42	31	9	2	106	25	71
1921	1st	42	35	6	1	91	24	76
1922	2nd	42	28	10	4	83	26	66
1923	1st	38	23	9	6	67	29	55
1924	1st	38	25	9	4	72	22	59
1925	1st	38	25	10	3	76	26	60
1926	6th	38	19	6	13	79	55	44
1927	1st	38	23	10	5	85	41	56
1928	1st	38	26	8	4	109	36	60
1929	1st	38	30	7	1	107	32	67
1930	1st	38	28	4	6	94	32	60
1931	1st	38	27	6	5	96	29	60
1932	2nd	38	28	5	5	118	42	61
1933	1st	38	26	10	2	113	43	62
1934	1st	38	30	6	2	118	41	66
1935	1st	38	25	5	8	96	46	55

SEASON ENDING	POS	P	W	D	L	F	A	Pts
1936	2nd	38	27	7	4	110	43	61
1937	1st	38	26	9	3	88	32	61
1938	3rd	38	18	13	7	75	49	49
1939	1st	38	25	9	4	112	55	59
1947	1st	30	21	4	5	76	26	46
1948	2nd	30	21	4	5	64	28	46
1949	1st	30	20	6	4	63	32	46
1950	1st	30	22	6	2	58	26	50
1951	2nd	30	17	4	9	64	37	38
1952	2nd	30	16	9	5	61	31	41
1953	1st	30	18	7	5	80	29	43
1954	4th	30	13	8	9	56	35	34
1955	3rd	30	19	8	1	67	33	41
1956	1st	34	22	8	4	85	27	52
1957	1st	34	26	3	5	96	48	55
1958	2nd	34	22	5	7	89	49	49
1959	1st	34	21	8	5	92	51	50
1960	3rd	34	17	8	9	72	38	42
1961	1st	34	23	5	6	88	46	51
1962	2nd	34	22	7	5	84	31	51
1963	1st	34	25	7	2	94	28	57
1964	1st	34	25	5	4	85	31	55
1965	5th	34	18	8	8	78	35	44
1966	2nd	34	25	5	4	91	29	55
1967	2nd	34	24	7	3	92	29	55
1968	2nd	34	28	5	1	93	34	61
1969	2nd	34	22	7	6	81	32	49

SEASON ENDING	POS	P	W	D	L	F	A	Pts
1970	2nd	34	19	7	8	67	40	45
1971	4th	34	16	9	9	58	34	41
1972	3rd	34	21	2	11	71	38	44
1973	2nd	34	26	4	4	74	30	56
1974	3rd	34	21	6	7	67	34	48
1975	1st	34	25	6	3	86	33	56
1976	1st	36	23	8	5	60	24	54
1977	2nd	36	18	10	8	62	37	46
1978	1st	36	24	7	5	76	39	55
1979	2nd	36	18	9	9	52	35	45
1980	5th	36	15	7	14	50	46	37
1981	3rd	36	16	12	8	60	32	44
1982	3rd	36	16	11	9	57	45	43
1983	4th	36	13	12	11	52	41	38
1984	4th	36	15	12	9	53	41	42
1985	4th	36	13	12	11	47	8	38
1986	5th	36	13	9	14	53	45	35
1987	1st	44	31	7	6	85	23	69
1988	3rd	44	26	8	10	85	34	60
1989	1st	36	26	4	6	62	26	56
1990	1st	36	20	11	5	48	19	51
1991	1st	36	24	7	5	62	23	55
1992	1st	44	33	6	5	101	31	72
1993	1st	44	33	7	4	97	35	73
1994	1st	44	22	14	8	74	41	58
1995	1st	36	20	9	7	60	35	69
1996	1st	36	27	6	3	85	25	87

SEASON ENDING	POS	P	W	D	L	F	A	Pts
1997	1st	36	25	5	6	85	33	80
1998	2nd	36	21	9	6	76	38	72
1999	1st	36	23	8	5	78	31	77
2000	1st	36	28	6	2	96	26	90
2001	2nd	38	26	4	8	76	36	82
2002	2nd	38	25	10	3	82	27	85
2003	1st	38	31	4	3	101	28	97
2004	2nd	38	31	5	2	105	25	98
2005	1st	38	29	6	3	78	22	93
2006	3rd	38	21	10	7	67	37	73
2007	2nd	38	21	9	8	61	32	72
2008	2nd	38	27	5	6	84	33	86
2009	1st	38	26	8	4	77	28	86
2010	1st	38	26	9	3	82	28	87
2011	1st	38	30	3	5	88	29	93
2012	2nd	38	26	5	7	77	28	73*
2013 (Division 3)	1st	36	25	8	3	87	29	83
2014 (League 1)	1st	36	33	3	0	106	18	102
2015 (Championship)	3rd	36	19	10	7	69	39	67
2016 (Championship)	1st	36	25	6	5	88	34	81
2017	3rd	38	19	10	9	56	44	67
2018	3rd	38	21	7	10	76	50	70
2019	2nd	38	23	9	6	82	27	78
2020	2nd	29	21	4	4	64	19	67**
2021	1st	38	32	6	0	92	13	102

*Rangers demoted to Division 3. ** Season curtailed due to Covid 19.

WALTER SMITH CELEBRATES
WINNING THE LEAGUE IN 2011

MANAGERS

Rangers have had more managers since the year 2000 than they had from 1899 to 2000. Dick Advocaat straddled the millennium taking charge from July 1998 to December 2001.

DICK ADVOCAAT

Since then Alec McLeish, Paul Le Guen, Ian Durrant, Walter Smith, Ally McCoist, Kenny McDowall, Stuart McCall, Mark Warburton, Graeme Murty, Pedro Caixinha, Jimmy Nicholl and Steven Gerrard have all taken charge for between a few days in the case of Durrant and Nicholl to four and a half years in the case of McLeish.

At the other end of the club's history, William Wilton took charge from 1899 to 1920 having previously been at the club since 1883, initially as a player. William Struth then took charge until 1954 when Scott Symon succeeded him until November 1967. He was replaced by David White who lasted two years before Willie Waddell took the hot-seat until May 1972.

In between the summer of 1972 and April 1986 Jock Wallace had two spells either side of playing legend John Greig managing the club between June 1978 and October 1983.

From April 1986 until the same month in 1991 Graeme Souness held the reins after which Walter Smith was manager for seven years before Dick Advocaat's arrival.

BELOW: JOCK WALLACE

McCOIST

Alistair Murdoch McCoist's place in Rangers folklore is secured by his stature as the club's record scorer. A phenomenal 355 goals consisted of 251 in the league, 21 in Europe, 54 in the League Cup and 29 in the Scottish Cup.

Ally won all but the last of his 61 Scotland caps whilst at Rangers who he went on to manage. Always a charismatic player with a natural charm, Ally remains an ever popular figure when covering games as a TV and radio pundit.

Born in Bellshill on 24 September 1962, his first opportunity at joining the club came as a schoolboy, but he declined the offer in order to sign for St Johnstone, subsequently turning professional with them in December 1978.

After making four appearances in 1978-79 and 15 the following season, all without scoring, Ally burst onto the scene with 22 goals in 38 appearances during the 1980-81 season.

Such goalscoring exploits attracted considerable attention from other clubs, with Rangers among those willing to pay what it took to get him to Ibrox, but Ally opted for a move south of the border to Sunderland, signing in a deal worth £350,000, then a huge sum for a player still in his teens. Defences in England proved harder to break down with Ally scoring just eight goals in his 56 appearances for the Roker Park club. McCoist finally made the move to Ibrox in June 1983, costing £185,000, in one of the best transfers ever pulled off by the club.

ALLY McCOIST
1988-89

ALLY CELEBRATES SCORING THE SECOND V LEEDS EUROPEAN CUP SECOND ROUND FIRST LEG 20/10/92

RIGHT: ALLY WITH THE 1997 PREMIER LEAGUE TROPHY

Ally's goalscoring helped Rangers win ten League titles, the League Cup on nine occasions and the Scottish Cup once (his medal haul in this competition might have been higher had he not suffered from injuries at the wrong times), whilst on a personal level he was the European Golden Boot winner in 1992 and 1993 and named Player of the Year in 1992. His tally of goals also included an astonishing 28 hat-tricks, another club record.

His 19 goals for Scotland included one at Ibrox against Malta in 1993 and climaxed with the only goal of the game against Switzerland at Euro 96.

From June 2011 until four days before Christmas in 2014, Ally managed Rangers, winning 121 of his 167 games and winning back-to-back promotions in 2013 and 2014 as he gallantly led Rangers in perhaps the most difficult era in the club's long and proud history.

McGREGOR

Born in Edinburgh on 31 January 1982 Allan McGregor came to Rangers from Hutchison Vale in 1998 and made his first-team debut in a 6-0 Scottish Cup win at Forfar Athletic on 24 February 2002. With Billy Dodds scoring a hat-trick that day when Rangers other scorers were Shota Arveladze and Andrei Kanchelskis, it illustrates how long Allan has been around.

Having made his first couple of league appearances later the same season, McGregor then waited until the season after next for another opportunity - coincidentally, again starting with a 6-0 cup win over Forfar, the first of six appearances in that 2003-04 campaign.

He went on loan to St. Johnstone in 2004-05 when he played 24 times before returning in January to get a couple of Premier League games with his parent club. The following season, another loan gave him the opportunity to play regular Premier football, this time with Dunfermline for whom he played 31 times.

Returning to Rangers, Allan established himself as first choice with 41 appearances in 2006-07. It was a season in which he made his European bow in the UEFA Cup and climaxed the campaign with an international debut and a clean sheet for good measure in Austria at the end of the season.

McGregor remained number one for the next five seasons during which time he won three SPL titles and four domestic cup winner's medals in addition to the four cup-winning squads he had been part of earlier in his Rangers career. Unfortunately, injury prevented him from being part of the side who played in the UEFA Cup final of 2008.

ALLAN POSES WITH THE 2021 PREMIERSHIP TROPHY ALONGSIDE STEVEN GERRARD

ALLAN SAVES A SHOOT-OUT PENALTY DURING THE 2008 CIS INSURANCE CUP FINAL WIN OVER DUNDEE UNITED

RIGHT: ALLAN V VFB STUTTGART CHAMPIONS LEAGUE 19/09/07

Following the liquidation of Rangers in 2012, McGregor moved on to Besiktas. Debuting with a clean sheet in a victory at Kardimir on 1 September 2012 Allan went on to play 27 times in his season in Turkey before joining Hull City for a reported £1.5m. Debuting at Chelsea four days after keeping goal for Scotland against England at Wembley, he went on to keep goal 147 times for the Tigers, one of which was in the FA Cup final against Arsenal at the end of his first season.

Relegated at the end of his second term, he missed only two Championship fixtures in his third year in England as Hull were promoted, before being loaned to Cardiff City in his fourth season as he recovered from injury.

With his parent club having been relegated again, McGregor once more played all but two Championship games in his final season at the KC Stadium in 2017-18 before rejecting a new contract and returning to Rangers in 2018.

Astonishingly, Allan has been even better in his second spell at Ibrox than he was in his first. Having to maintain concentration in a side that regularly dominate is a challenge for goalkeepers, but McGregor's magnificence is such that he is always on top of his game and when called upon, frequently makes telling and spectacular reaction saves.

As 2020-21 ended with another SPL title under his belt, Allan had taken his overall total of Rangers appearances to over 400 in a season when he was deservedly SPFL Premiership Player of the Year. He retired from international football in 2019 having won 42 caps for his country.

McNEIL

Even if Moses McNeil had achieved little or nothing of note on the field, he would still be assured a place in the club's history, for he was one of the original founding fathers who took a stroll through West End Park in Glasgow and came up with the idea of forming a football club. It was also Moses who came up with the name Rangers, spotting it in a book about an English rugby club and believed it to be the perfect name for their new football club.

Moses was born in Rhu on 29 October 1855 and was one of seven brothers, of whom four were to go on to play for Rangers, with Moses being joined by Peter, Harry and William. Only James, John and Alec never played for the club, but they would certainly have taken an interest in the exploits of their younger brothers, especially when Moses went on to become the first Rangers player to earn international honours, appearing in Scotland's 4-0 win over Wales in Glasgow in March 1876.

MOSES McNEIL 1876

Four years later, Moses earned his second and final cap for his country, a 4-5 defeat in Glasgow at the hands of England.

Tough tackling and tricky as a winger, Moses was to also appear in two Scottish Cup finals for Rangers, both against Vale of Leven, losing after a replay in 1877 and finishing level in 1879 - Rangers refused to play in the replay and lost by default! Thereafter his appearances for the club became sporadic, with his last coming in a friendly against Aston Villa in March 1882, after which he concentrated on his profession as a commercial traveller and died in 1938.

BOB MCPHAIL 1935

McPHAIL

Bob McPhail was born in Barrhead and first came to prominence with Airdrie, helping them win the Scottish Cup in 1924 whilst aged just 18. It was to begin a love affair with the competition for Bob, for he went on to collect a further six winners' medals.

His performances for Airdrie, displaying a coolness in front of goal that belied his tender years did not go unnoticed by Rangers and in 1927 they paid £5,000, then a considerable fee, to bring him to Ibrox. He was to form an uncanny partnership with Alan Morton and later Davie Kinnear on the left wing, but it was his ability to gel with fellow strikers Sam English and Jimmy Smith that proved most beneficial.

Bob was to score a total of 230 League goals for the club, a record figure that was to survive nearly sixty years before being overtaken by Ally McCoist, having previously scored 70 for Airdrie.

Aside from his seven Scottish Cup medals, Bob was also to collect nine League titles and 17 caps for Scotland, scoring seven goals.

The outbreak of the Second World War effectively brought his Rangers career to an end, although he did make a number of wartime appearances for both Rangers (adding a further three goals to his tally) and St Mirren before retiring in 1941. He later had a spell as reserve team trainer at Ibrox.

MEIKLEJOHN

Davie was born in Govan in 1900, joined Rangers from Maryhill Juniors and made his debut in the 2-0 win over Aberdeen in March 1920, going on to help the club win the League title at the end of the season having made ten appearances and scored two goals.

It was to be the first of no fewer than twelve League titles won whilst at Ibrox over the next sixteen years, and for good measure Davie also collected five winners' medals in the Scottish Cup, scoring one of Rangers' goals from the penalty spot in the 4-0 win against Celtic in 1928 having lost on his two previous final appearances.

Davie also won 15 caps for Scotland, captaining the side twice, and was respected throughout the game. He also received considerable credit from all sections of the media for his actions in the infamous clash with Celtic in 1931 when Celtic goalkeeper John Thomson was accidentally killed diving at the feet of Sam English; it was Davie who recognised the seriousness of the situation, beckoning the medical staff to attend to the stricken player and silencing a section of the Rangers crowd who had begun barracking the fallen player.

He remained a Rangers player until 1936 when he retired from playing and went to work for the newspaper The Daily Record. Davie was lured back to football after the war, becoming Partick Thistle manager in 1947. He collapsed and died on 22 August 1959 whilst in the directors' box at Broomfield.

MORELOS WITH THE MATCHBALL AFTER HIS HAT-TRICK IN THE 6-0 WIN OVER ST JOSEPH'S, 18 JULY 2019

MORELOS

Colombian international Alfredo Morelos had won top-flight titles with both of his previous clubs in Columbia and Finland before adding an SPFL medal with Rangers in the joyous 55th title winning season of 2021.

Costing a reported £1m in 2017 after scoring 46 goals in 62 games across two seasons in Finland with HJK, Morelos made his Rangers debut in the Europa League away to Progres Niederkorn of Luxembourg.

MORELOS SCORES THE SECOND GOAL IN THE 4-1 SPL WIN OVER CELTIC, 2 MAY 2021

He scored his first goals with a brace against Dunfermline on his fourth appearance. That signalled the start of a sequence of eight goals in six games as Alfredo demonstrated Rangers had acquired a regular goalscorer.

He ended his first campaign in Scotland with 18 goals, but really made an impact in his second season when a total haul of 31 included his first international goal as Columbia beat Peru 1-0 at the end of a goal-laden season, which also included a four-goal haul against Kilmarnock and a hat-trick away to the same club.

CELEBRATIONS AFTER HIS GOAL AGAINST CELTIC, 2 MAY 2021

Unfortunately, the season also brought no fewer than five red cards as Morelos struggled to keep his emotions in check.

There were two more reds in the Covid 19 affected 2019-20 season, but the goals kept coming as well, 29 of them, including a Europa League hat-trick.

Perhaps significantly, as he helped Steven Gerrard's side to the title in 2020-21, Morelos managed to avoid any red cards, but scored 17 goals taking his Rangers tally to 94, including 23 in Europe which made him Rangers top European goal-scorer

MORTON

Alan Morton served Rangers for over fifty years and is rightly regarded as one of the most important men in the club's history. His portrait stands at the top of the marble staircase in the Main Stand.

Born in Glasgow in 1893, Morton began his career with Queen's Park and was targeted by Rangers by new manager Bill Struth as his first signing after taking over in 1920. Alan was persuaded to turn professional (albeit on a part-time basis) and join Rangers, making his debut against Airdrie in August 1920.

Alan's final appearance in a Rangers shirt was also against Airdrie, in January 1933. In between Alan made 495 first-team appearances, of which 382 were in the League and scored 166 goals (115 in the League).

It was his ability to create chances, however, which earned him the everlasting affection of both Rangers and Scotland followers, most notably in the famous 1928 clash between England and Scotland at Wembley. Scotland produced a sparkling 5-1 win, with Alan providing three crosses for Huddersfield's Alec Jackson to convert.

During the match an English fan described him as a 'wee blue devil' and the nickname was applied to Alan thereafter. Winner of nine League championships and one Scottish Cup winners' medal, in 1930. Twenty-nine of his 31 caps came whilst associated with Rangers and he also represented the Scottish League on 15 occasions.

Alan combined his playing career with being a mining engineer. When the end came to his playing career in 1933, he did not sever all links with Rangers, being appointed to the board of directors and continued to serve the club in this capacity until his death in 1971.

His impact on the game, already legendary for his exploits on the field, was permanently assured thanks to his contributions as a sports administrator off it.

NEGRI

When Marco Negri arrived at Ibrox in the summer of 1997 for £3.5 million from Perugia, he was seen as the obvious replacement for an ageing Ally McCoist. Marco certainly started in blistering form, setting a new Scottish Premier League record of netting in ten consecutive matches, with his tally including a haul of five against Dundee United and four against Dunfermline Athletic.

Marco (born in Milan on 27 October 1970) ended his first season at Rangers with 33 League goals in 28 appearances, although it wasn't enough to win the title, which went to Celtic. He also scored only one goal in the Scottish Cup, which went to Hearts, and none at all in the League Cup, also won by Celtic.

Despite his goals, Marco appeared to be a complex character, preferring to celebrate his numerous goals with a simple handshake.

A serious eye injury ruled Negri out of the 1998-99 season after which he appeared just three times in the following two seasons before leaving the club with a total of 36 goals from his 40+3 games.

Having been loaned to Vicenza in 1999 Marco made a handful of appearances for Bologna, Cagliari and Perugia as well as netting eight goals in 20 games for his penultimate club Livorno. Earlier in his career he had started at Udinese and played for Ternana, Cosenza and Perugia as well as having lengthy loans with Novara and Bologna.

NUMAN WITH THE 2003 SCOTTISH FA CUP
AFTER THE 1-0 VICTORY OVER DUNDEE

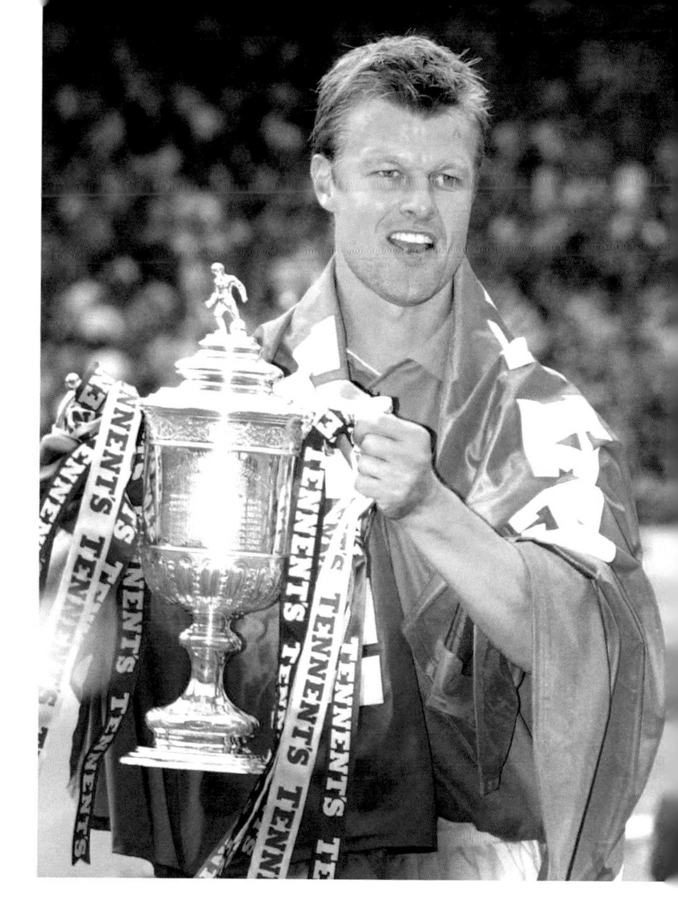

NUMAN

Born in Heemskerk on 14 December 1969, Arthur Numan was Rangers' manager Dick Advocaat's first signing when taking over at Ibrox in 1998, Advocaat returning to his former club PSV Eindhoven to pay £4.5 million for a player who had established a reputation as one of the best full-backs in the Dutch game.

Arthur began his career with amateur club SV Beverwijk before being spotted by Haarlem, where coach Advocaat switched him from an attacking midfield player to a full-back. It was this switch that turned him into one of the best defenders in the Dutch game, prompting a move to FC Twente in 1991.

Made captain of the club Arthur also skippered the Dutch Under-21 side before earning a big money move to PSV Eindhoven. In October 1992 he was awarded his first full cap for his country, where Advocaat was coach.

By the time the curtain came down on his international career, he had 45 caps to his name and had helped Holland finish fourth in the 1998 World Cup in which he played in the quarter-final against Argentina.

That summer he joined Rangers, following his former manager and coach Advocaat to Ibrox. The season started promisingly enough, with victory in the League Cup over St Johnstone, but although the League title was won, Arthur made only eight appearances during the course of the season owing to injury. He returned the following campaign, which saw the League and Scottish Cup double success and was the captain that lifted the trophy after Aberdeen had been beaten in the Scottish Cup final.

NUMAN GETS THE BETTER OF CELTIC'S HENRIK LARSSON, 2001

Arthur was to collect a further five winners' medals during his time at Ibrox, with double cup success in 2001-02 being followed by a domestic clean sweep the following term. This proved to be the final season for Arthur, who announced his retirement from playing at the end of the season. Despite overtures from Villarreal of Spain, Arthur remained true to his word, preferring to pursue a new career in the media before becoming team manager of the Netherlands B team in 2008 and going on to scout for Aston Villa.

A POLICE OFFICER CHECKS THE TIME AT THE START OF THE MATCH BETWEEN ARCH RIVALS RANGERS AND CELTIC, 1949

OLD FIRM

Rangers against Celtic is one of the most fiercely contested fixtures in world football. Whilst the fixture was seen as a straight battle between Protestant and Catholic clubs for many years, the lines between each club's ideologies have become blurred in recent years, leaving a fixture that has once again become all about football, nothing more and nothing less.

Whilst the two clubs might be referred to as the best of enemies today, it wasn't always the case. Indeed, relations between the two clubs were for many years extremely cordial, with Rangers providing the opposition in what was Celtic's very first match, in May 1888.

Unsure of the quality of the opposition that would face them, Rangers selected eleven players that were a mixture of established first-teamers, a handful of reserves and one or two guests.

Despite this combination Celtic proved too strong on the day, winning 5-2. The first goal in the match was scored by Neilly Mccallum of Celtic, who a few months earlier had turned out for Rangers in a friendly fixture against Aston Villa and thus became the first player to have turned out for both sides of the Glasgow divide.

After the match the two sides, together with club officials, sat down together for a supper and concert at St Mary's Hall.

A POLICEMAN GIVES ADVICE TO A FAN AT THE OLD FIRM CLASH, 1949

Three months later in August 1888 the two sides met again, with Rangers getting their revenge with a 9-1 victory, although this was still a match that fell into the category of Rangers providing the opposition for their much younger rivals from across the city.

The first Scottish Cup meeting between the two sides came in the first round in September 1890, with Celtic winning 1-0. In October 1888, the two clubs met in the quarter-final of the Glasgow Cup, with Celtic coming to Ibrox and recording a 6-1 victory, still their biggest ever win at Ibrox.

Celtic could also claim to have got the better of their rivals in the first League meetings between the two sides, played the same season, with a 2-2 draw at Parkhead being followed by a 2-1 win for Celtic at Ibrox. Rangers, however, had the last laugh, finishing joint top of the table with Dumbarton and being declared joint champions after the two sides had drawn a deciding match.

The two sides had to wait until February 1894 before they met in the Scottish Cup Final for the first time, with Rangers registering a 3-1 win to lift the trophy for the very first time, making the victory over Celtic especially sweet.

It was not until 1898 that the relationship between Rangers and Celtic began to become strained. A crowd of 50,000 was packed into Parkhead for the New Year's Day meeting between the top two sides in the League, with the 40 or so policemen on duty unable to prevent frequent invasions by the crowd.

ALFIE CONN PLAYED FOR RANGERS BEFORE APPEARING FOR CELTIC

RIGHT: RANGERS FANS AT CELTIC, MAY 1999

The match itself was finely balanced at 1-1 when another invasion after seventy minutes proved impossible to clear, with the game subsequently being abandoned. Although Celtic came in for considerable criticism over their inability to control their fans, Rangers were more aggrieved over Celtic's refusal to share the gate money 50/50, as had supposedly been agreed, and received only 20%, their allotted share under the regulations of the time.

Following the Ibrox disaster of 1902, Rangers organised a four team competition involving them, Celtic, Sunderland and Everton in what became billed as the British League Cup. The trophy for the competition was the Exhibition Cup, a trophy that had been won by Rangers in 1901 after an eight team competition, beating Celtic in the final.

The two Glasgow rivals met in the final of the British League Cup, with Celtic winning 3-2 after extra time, but what caused the controversy between the two sides was Celtic's refusal to put the trophy, which Rangers believed was rightfully theirs, up for annual competition. The trophy, the cause of much aggravation in 1902, remains at Parkhead to this day.

Whilst the two sides learned to tolerate each other in the years that followed, at least as far as the respective officials were concerned, the same could not be said for followers of either side. The League meeting in 1898, which as noted earlier was subsequently abandoned, was just the first in a number of matches that were disrupted, either during or after by invasions and serious and violent clashes.

MO JOHNSTON PLAYED FOR CELTIC FIRST BEFORE LATER JOINING RANGERS

After the 1980 Scottish Cup Final, which Celtic won 1-0 after extra time at Hampden Park. When the Celtic players went over to the end where their fans were congregated to celebrate, hoards of Rangers fans invaded the pitch and engaged in bitter battle on the pitch against their foes.

Although both clubs were subsequently fined (a paltry £20,000 each), legislation was introduced in the shape of the Criminal Justice (Scotland) Act 1980 that went some considerable way to removing the stain of crowd violence from the Scottish game.

Whilst there were several examples of players appearing for Rangers and then Celtic, with Alfie Conn during the 1970s being one of the most celebrated examples, instances of a player appearing for Celtic and then Rangers are much rarer.

Much of the reason for this was the religious background of the players - Celtic would sign a player irrespective of his religion, whilst for many years Rangers would only sign Protestant players. All this changed with the controversial (at least as far as Rangers fans were concerned) signing of Maurice 'Mo' Johnston.

If the religious overtones to the fixture have been removed, the intensity of the rivalry has not diminished. If anything it has increased; the pressure to finish the season ahead of their greatest rivals is still one that drives both Rangers and Celtic on to bigger and better things. Rangers, both inside and outside the club, still dream of emulating their rivals and getting to lift the European Champions Cup, the holy grail of club football.

STEVEN DAVIS

PLAYER OF THE YEAR

The Scottish Football Writers Association introduced their Player of the Year award in 1965, with Celtic's Billy McNeill the very first winner. The following Rangers players have won the award.

BARRY FERGUSON

1966	John Greig
1972	Dave Smith
1975	Sandy Jardine
1976	John Greig
1978	Derek Johnstone
1989	Richard Gough
1992	Ally McCoist
1993	Andy Goram
1994	Mark Hateley
1995	Brian Laudrup
1996	Paul Gascoigne
1997	Brian Laudrup
2000	Barry Ferguson
2003	Barry Ferguson
2008	Carlos Cuellar
2010	David Weir
2021	Steven Davis

The players' union, the PFA, instigated its own award in 1978, voted for by all professional players. The following Rangers players have won the award.

1978	Derek Johnstone,
1992	Ally McCoist
1993	Andy Goram
1994	Mark Hately
1995	Brian Laudrup
1996	Paul Gascoigne
2002	Lorenzo Amoruso
2003	Barry Ferguson
2005	Fernando Ricksen (jointly with John Hartson of Celtic)
2010	Steven Davis
2021	James Tavernier

PROVAN

Born in Falkirk on 11 March 1941, Davie Provan seemed set for a lengthy and successful career at Rangers until a horrific broken leg brought his Ibrox career to an end, even if it wasn't the end of his playing career.

Davie had had to wait five years before he made his Rangers debut and it was the unfortunate broken leg sustained by Eric Caldow whilst on national duty that gave Davie his opening, appearing in the 3-1 win over Hibernian in April 1963. Davie made steady progress thereafter, winning five caps for Scotland and collecting one League title, three Scottish Cups and two League Cup winners' medals, including the treble in 1964 and also appearing in the unsuccessful European Cup Winners' Cup final of 1967.

That September, in the first Old Firm clash of the season, he suffered a broken leg in a challenge from Bertie Auld and was out of the side until December 1968. Although he returned to make eight appearances for the club, taking his tally up to 262, he was not the player he had been prior to his injury and was allowed to leave Ibrox, heading for England and Crystal Palace.

DAVID PROVAN, BACK ROW CENTRE

Davie made only one appearance for the Eagles before moving on to Plymouth Argyle in March 1971 and made 129 appearances for the West Country side. He then returned to Scotland to finish his career with St Mirren.

Whilst it may have been a clash with Bertie Auld that effectively ended Davie's Ibrox career, Davie himself never bore any malice, with the pair subsequently becoming good pals and regular partners on the golf course.

PRSO

Miladin Prso, known as Dado, was born in Zadar in Croatia on 5 November 1974. He began his career with NK Zadar in 1991, had spells with Hajduk Split and NK Pazinka and was regarded as a competent if not spectacular striker.

All that was to change with his arrival in France in 1993, joining FC Rouen and two years later moving on to San Raphael. It was AS Monaco manager Jean Tigana who spotted talents in Dado that other managers had missed, signing him in 1996 and sending him out on loan to AC Ajaccio in order to get him fitter for the role he had in mind.

Dado returned to Monaco in 1999 and proved a revelation, helping the club win the French title and impress in the Champions League, Dado's personal highlight being a four-goal haul in an 8-3 win over Deportivo la Coruna before he played as a substitute in the final as his side went down to Jose Mourinho's Porto.

That summer he scored against France in the European Championships after which he joined Rangers where he linked up effectively with Nacho Novo. The pair notched 37 goals between them as the league title was won, Dado's 18-goal haul being added to by two more as he helped Rangers to win the League Cup.

Croatian Footballer of the Year in three successive seasons from 2003, Dado won three of his 32 caps at the 2006 FIFA World Cup and retired from football a year later due to knee injuries. At his final Ibrox appearance he was given a 'Guard of Honour' by his teammates. He had scored 37 times in 123 games he played in such style.

QUOTES

"To be a Ranger is to sense the sacred trust of upholding all that such a name means in this shrine of football. They must be true in their conception of what the Ibrox tradition seeks from them. No true Ranger has ever failed in the tradition set him."

Bill Struth

"I was presented with the trophy in an ante-room in the bowels of the Nou Camp. You could say it was an anti-climax."

John Greig on the 1972 European Cup Winners' Cup final.

"Sorry Mr Chairman, but this is the earliest I have been late for some time."

Ally McCoist turns up late for the chairman.

"If I have one regret about my career, it is that I did not join Rangers a lot sooner."

Ray Wilkins

ALLY McCOIST

"Our very success, gained you will agree by skill, will draw more people than ever to see it. And that will benefit many more clubs than Rangers. Let the others come after us. We welcome the chase. It is healthy for us. We will never hide from it. Never fear, inevitably we shall have our years of failure, and when they arrive, we must reveal tolerance and sanity. No matter the days of anxiety that come our way, we shall emerge stronger because of the trials to be overcome. That has been the philosophy of the Rangers since the days of the gallant pioneers."

Bill Struth

MARCOS NEGRI BELOW: **BILL STRUTH**

"I am of Rangers and I'll stay of Rangers until I die."

Bill Struth

Manager for 34 years and director for a further two years until his death.

"There are people for whom Rangers Football Club is their entire way of life."

Walter Smith

"What do I like about Rangers? I like winning."

Mark Hateley

"Glasgow Rangers. God I loved playing for them"

Paul Gascoigne

"Gazza said he was taking his wallet out on the pitch with him. I didn't understand what he was talking about until he told me that he'd read something in a paper that my mother said I would either be a footballer or a thief."

Marcos Negri

"I have been lucky, lucky in those who were around me from the boardroom to the dressing-room. In time of stress, their unstinted support, unbroken devotion to our club and calmness in adversity eased the task of making Rangers FC the premier club in this country."

Bill Struth

RECORDS

TORE ANDRE FLO

RECORD VICTORY

14-2 v Blairgowrie
Scottish Cup first round · 20/01/1934

RECORD DEFEAT

0-6 v Dumbarton
Scottish League · 04/05/1892

MOST LEAGUE POINTS

98 in Scottish Premier League · 2003-04
(three points for a win)

76 in Scottish League · 1920-21
(two points for a win)

MOST LEAGUE GOALS

118 in Scottish League · 1931-32 and 1933-34

MOST GOALS IN A SEASON

Jim Forrest · 57 · 1964-65

MOST GOALS IN ALL COMPETITIONS

Ally McCoist 355 1983-1998

MOST APPEARANCES IN ALL COMPETITIONS

John Greig · 755 · 1961-1978

MOST CAPPED PLAYER

Ally McCoist · 60 appearances for Scotland

RECORD TRANSFER FEE RECEIVED

£9m · Alan Hutton from Spurs · 2008

RECORD TRANSFER FEE PAID

£12.5m · Tore Andre Flo to Chelsea · 2000

ROBERTSON

Born in Dumbarton on 25 February 1877, wing-half Jacky Robertson began his playing career with Morton before being spotted by Everton and signed with the Goodison Park club in 1897.

He made 26 appearances in the First Division, scoring one goal but found the pace a little above him and so switched to Southampton of the Southern League the following year.

He returned to Scotland in 1899, signing with champions Rangers and made his debut against Clyde in August 1899, helping the club retain the title at the end of the season. Jacky would go on to make 120 first-team appearances, winning League title medals in 1900 and 1901 and the Scottish Cup in 1903 as well as runners-up medals in 1904 and 1905.

First capped by Scotland whilst on the books of Everton, he went on to make 16 appearances for his country, 14 of which were whilst with Rangers. He was captain of the side in their 4-1 defeat of England in 1900, a match in which Scotland wore the primrose and pink racing colours of racehorse owner Archibald Philip Primrose, Lord Rosebery. After the match Lord Rosebery was heard to remark to Jacky 'I have never seen my colours so well sported since Ladas won the Derby.'

In 1905, Jacky accepted an invitation to become player-manager of the new Chelsea Football Club as they kicked off their campaign in the Second Division. Jacky made 36 appearances over the next two years before switching to Glossop in a similar capacity. Jacky then went to Europe to coach MTK Budapest and Rapid Vienna. He died in 1935.

SHAW

Jock Shaw, Aptly known as 'Tiger', had a biting tackle and an uncompromising style that made him a feared opponent, with his fitness and speed off the mark making up for any shortcomings in his height (he stood just 5' 7") and weight (11 stone).

He was already considered the finished article at full-back when Bill Struth swooped on Airdrie to pay £2,000 to bring Jock to Ibrox in July 1938, appearing in all but two of Rangers' League matches during the 1938-39 season as the League title was won.

The outbreak of the Second World War caused the abandonment of the Scottish League the following campaign but Jock helped Rangers win the hastily arranged Scottish Regional League Western Division and Emergency War Cup that term.

Jock would go on to help Rangers win all seven wartime Leagues and a total of five cup competitions and was still the club's first choice left-back when normal League football resumed in 1946, with Rangers winning the League and also the newly introduced League Cup, the latter with a 4-0 victory over Aberdeen in April 1947.

That same month Jock won the first of his four caps for Scotland, captaining the side in the 1-1 draw with England at Wembley (he was captain for all four of his appearances).

Jock would go on to win a total of four Scottish League titles, three Scottish Cups and two League Cups, figures that included the first domestic treble, achieved in 1949, and a double the following year, with only defeat in the final of the League Cup robbing Rangers of back to back trebles.

Jock was already 38 years of age when the double was won and continued playing until he was 42 before switching to coaching and heading up Rangers' third team.

Over the years Jock was responsible for grooming future Rangers stars such as John Greig, Sandy Jardine and Willie Henderson. He later became groundsman for the club.

SMITH
NICOL

Born on 25 December 1873, Nicol Smith was spotted by Rangers whilst on international duty for the junior side against Ireland in 1893 and signed up almost immediately. He was given a first-team debut by Rangers soon after, selected to play at full-back in place of the injured Donald Gow and did so well Gow was unable to get his place back in the side, prompting his departure for pastures new.

Nicol meanwhile formed an uncanny understanding with fellow full-back Jock Drummond, the pair proving to be one of the best full-back partnerships the club has ever had, helping Rangers win four League titles, three Scottish Cups (including Rangers' first in the competition) and winners' medals from the Glasgow Cup, Charity Cup, Glasgow League and Exhibition Cup, these competitions being significantly more important then than they might appear now.

Nicol and Drummond transferred their understanding from club to international level, winning 25 caps for Scotland between them.

In November 1904 Nicol made his last appearance for the club before being struck down with enteric fever. His wife contracted the disease whilst nursing him and was to die just before Christmas, with Nicol suffering a relapse from the disease on 4th January and dying two days later, leaving five children orphans. The club organised a benefit match for the children, which. raised nearly £400, but really the match was a chance for Rangers to say farewell to the 'Darvel Marvel'.

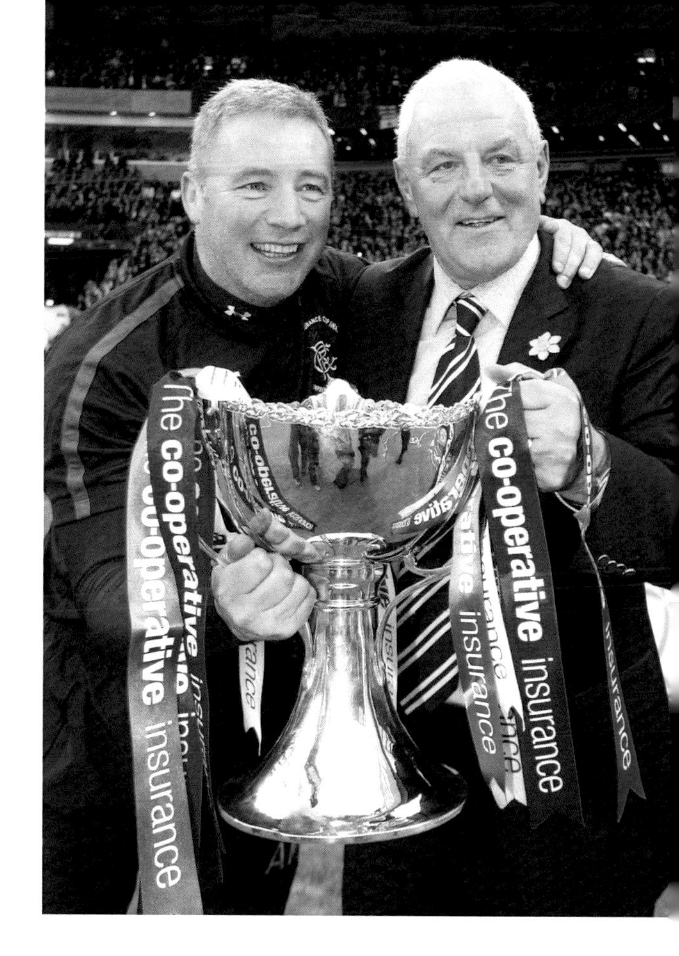

WALTER SMITH CELEBRATES WITH ASSISTANT MANAGER ALLY MCCOIST AND THE TROPHY AFTER THE 2011 CIS CUP FINAL VICTORY OVER CELTIC

SMITH
WALTER

Walter Smith was born in Carmyle on 24 February 1948 and dreamed of playing for Rangers as a youngster, although he didn't make the grade and so pursued his playing career with Dundee United whilst working part-time as an electrician.

After nine years at United he moved on to Dumbarton in 1975 but returned to Dundee United two years later. A pelvic injury threatened his playing career and he was encouraged by United manager Jim McLean to pursue a coaching career.

Eventually he was appointed assistant manager to Jim McLean whilst also working with the Scotland Under-18 side, guiding them to victory in the European Youth Championship in 1982. From there he became coach to the Under-21 side and served as Alex Ferguson's assistant during the 1986 World Cup in Mexico.

That April he got a call to become Graeme Souness's assistant at Ibrox, a position he readily accepted, even though he was on the board of directors at Tannadice.

He was to work with Graeme for some five years, the partnership bringing four League titles and four League Cups to Ibrox in that time. When Graeme left to join Liverpool, the Rangers board had no hesitation in offering the position of manager to Walter Smith.

Whilst assistant managers often find the step up to manager a difficult one to make, Walter took to the job immediately. By the time he resigned in 1998, he had become one of the club's most successful managers of all time, having lifted seven League titles, including the all important one that enabled them to register 'nine in a row' and numerous victories in the Scottish Cup and League Cup.

The 1992-93 season was undoubtedly the highlight, with all three domestic trophies lifted and Rangers coming to within one match of reaching the UEFA Champions League final. After leaving Rangers Walter resurfaced as manager of Everton in the FA Premier League, but continuing financial constraints at Goodison Park made it difficult to build a side to challenge for honours and he left the club in March 2002. Two years later he resumed his partnership with Alex Ferguson at Manchester United, but in December 2004 accepted the position of manager of the Scottish national team. Although he failed to take them into the 2006 World Cup Finals, he did give them back some pride and hope for the future with their performances.

A JUBILANT WALTER SMITH AFTER THE 2010 CIS INSURANCE CUP FINAL WIN OVER ST MIRREN

SOUNESS IN ACTION
V DUNFERMLINE, APRIL 1990

SOUNESS

Born in Edinburgh on 6 May 1953, Graeme Souness began his playing career at Spurs but made just one substitute appearance for the club in a UEFA Cup tie. A mixture of homesickness and his own desire for first-team action quicker prompted a move to Middlesbrough where he quickly established himself as one of the brightest midfield talents in the game.

SOUNESS 1987-88

He moved on to Liverpool for £350,000 in January 1978 and would go on to help the club win the League five times, the League Cup four times and the European Cup three times. In 1984 he was sold to Sampdoria for £650,000 and spent two seasons in Serie A before being lined up as player-manager of Rangers, arriving at the club in April 1986.

Right from the off, Graeme announced his intention of doing things his own way, going for the best players, irrespective at times of the cost and later of their religious backgrounds - if Rangers wanted to be the best, they had to attract the best players, with a number of England internationals eventually finding their way to Ibrox.

His first match in charge, away at Hibernian in the opening game of the 1986-87 season was a fiery affair, with Graeme getting sent off for a violent foul and beginning a love hate relationship with Scottish referees that was only partially brought to an end when he retired from playing during the 1989-90 season.

After a hesitant start to the 1986-87 campaign Rangers made progress up the table, bolstered by the arrival of the likes of Chris Woods, Graham Roberts and Terry Butcher and by the end of the campaign had won the League title for the first time in nine years and added the League Cup to the trophy cabinet.

There were other trophies too, with Graeme's time at Ibrox resulting in four League titles and four League Cups, only the Scottish FA Cup proving elusive with defeat in the final of 1988-89 the closest they came during this time.

As well as Woods, Roberts and Butcher, other England international players who signed for Rangers were Trevor Francis, Trevor Steven, Gary Stevens and Ray Wilkins, alongside others who had plied their trade in the English game such as Mark Falco and Richard Gough. This reversed the trend of previous decades when the best Scottish players had headed south of the border to play.

It was the signing of Mo Johnston that astonished the most, with Rangers seemingly signing a Catholic player for the first time in their history, but whilst Rangers under Graeme Souness were winning honours, who was to argue?

In 1988 Graeme was instrumental in bringing David Murray into the club, pairing up with the millionaire to buy a controlling interest in Rangers. Despite his vested interest in Rangers, there were still those who believed his heart was still at Liverpool and when, in April 1991 his former club invited him to take over as manager, he jumped at the chance. Later events were to prove he may have made the wrong decision, and subsequent appointments at Southampton, Galatasaray, Torino, Benfica, Blackburn Rovers and Newcastle United brought two trophies to Galatasaray and the 2002 League Cup to Blackburn.

PLAYER/MANAGER GRAEME SOUNESS CELEBRATES WINNING THE 1989 SCOTTISH PREMIER LEAGUE TITLE

Whilst he may have left Rangers too early into his managerial career, there is no doubt Graeme was almost single-handedly responsible for dragging the club back on to the top table of Scottish football. Had he remained at Ibrox for longer, he may even have converted consistent domestic success into European glory. His heart and Liverpool ensured we will never know.

A member of the Rangers and Scotland Halls of Fame, since ending his managerial career in 2007, Souness headed a consortium which tried to take over Wolves and has since become a TV pundit.

COLIN STEIN, 1975

STEIN

Born in Philipstoun in West Lothian on 10 May 1947, Colin Stein began his career with Hibernian and quickly developed into one of the best centre forwards in the Scottish game, prompting considerable attention from a number of other clubs.

Everton believed they had got their man with a £90,000 offer in October 1968, but Rangers were able to hijack this deal, paying £100,000 eyen though a number of Hibernian directors were not prepared to sell their star player to a rival Scottish club.

Their fears were to be proved right, for a week after netting a hat-trick on his debut against Arbroath, Colin netted a second hat-trick against his old club in a 6-1 victory, the presence of Colin adding some 20,000 to the gate.

For many years it was believed that the equalising goal he scored against Celtic on New Year's Day 1971 was indirectly responsible for causing the crush that left 66 dead, the inference being that those who were trying to leave the ground heard the roar of the crowd acclaiming the goal and turned back to see the celebrations, but later evidence showed all of those who died did so some considerable time after the final whistle.

Whilst Rangers were a struggling force domestically during Colin's time with the club, he was one of the key players who brought the European Cup Winners' Cup to Ibrox in 1972, scoring one of the goals in the 3-2 win over Dinamo Moscow. That proved to be a virtual swansong for Colin, for he was sold to Coventry City for £90,000 in October 1972. He made 83 appearances for the Highfield Road club, scoring 22 goals, before returning to Ibrox for a second spell in February 1975.

COLIN STEIN GETS AWAY FROM CELTIC'S KENNY DALGLISH, OCTOBER 1975

Whilst his initial games were not as goal laden as his first, he did score some vital strikes, including the one that clinched the title with a 1-1 draw against Hibernian. The following season, 1975-76 he collected his second League Cup winners' medal (he had been a member of the 1970-71 side) with a 1-0 victory over Celtic, the only domestic medals he got his hands on. Competition for places was at its keenest and he was allowed to go on loan to Kilmarnock during the 1977-78 campaign, eventually leaving Rangers at the end of the season. He won 21 caps for Scotland, all but four whilst with Rangers, and scored ten goals.

BILL STRUTH, 1924

STRUTH

Bill Struth was already working at Ibrox as a trainer when the tragic death of William Wilton was announced. The club decided on as painless a transition at Ibrox as was possible and appointed Bill to the position of secretary-manager in May 1920, a position he was to hold for the next 34 years.

Born in Edinburgh in 1873, he had been a stonemason and professional athlete before pursuing an interest in sports training, joining Clyde FC as trainer in 1908 and then switching to Ibrox in a similar capacity in 1914. Neither William Wilton nor Bill Struth worried much about tactics, but whilst Wilton was the club's father figure, Bill Struth imposed the discipline.

He established a network of scouts around the country, a network whose job it was to inform him of any players the club might be interested in signing and any gossip relating to those they had already signed.

BILL STRUTH, FORMER SECRETARY WHO IS BURIED CLOSE TO HIS BELOVED CLUB AT CRAIGTON CEMETERY

And whilst William Wilton had introduced a dress code into the club, it was Bill Struth who saw to it that it was enforced.

According to legend, he would look out of the window of his flat that overlooked Copland Road observing the players arriving for training - if even one arrived with his hands in his pockets, he would be summoned to the office and told to walk the street again, this time with his hands by his side.

Whilst the discipline within the club was strict, the rewards were great. Bill Struth insisted on the best of everything for Rangers, which meant travelling first class to every fixture and the best hotels and rooms when staying overnight. He himself kept numerous suits in his office and would sometimes change them three times a day.

This attention to detail brought with it immense success - eighteen League titles, including a then unprecedented five in a row between 1927 and 1931.

It was Bill Struth who delivered the club's first 'double' in 1928 and the first treble in 1949. He was appointed a director of the club in 1947, adding this role to that of secretary-manager.

He maintained this role until his resignation as secretary-manager in the summer of 1954, but remained on the board until his death, aged 81, in September 1956.

JAMES POSES WITH THE TROPHY AS HE CELEBRATES WINNING THE 2021 SCOTTISH PREMIERSHIP

TAVERNIER

Bradford born James Tavernier came to Rangers in 2015 and completed the triumphant 55th title year of 2020-21 having amassed 285+4 appearances and 65 goals, 46 of these games and 19 of the goals coming in 2020-21.

JAMES CELEBRATES SCORING V GALATASARAY, OCTOBER 2020

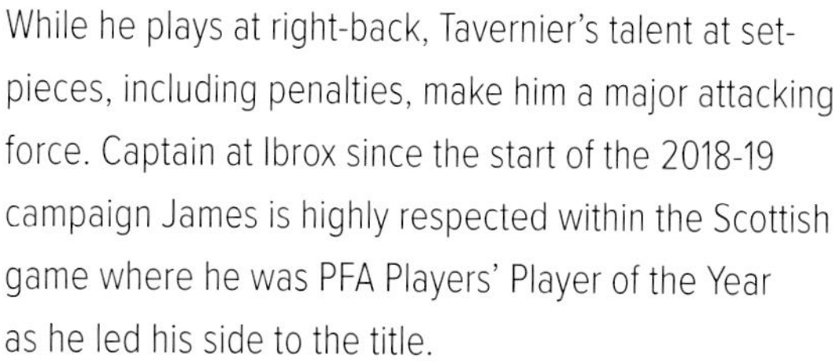

While he plays at right-back, Tavernier's talent at set-pieces, including penalties, make him a major attacking force. Captain at Ibrox since the start of the 2018-19 campaign James is highly respected within the Scottish game where he was PFA Players' Player of the Year as he led his side to the title.

A League Cup runner-up in 2020, he won the Championship and Challenge Cup as well as being Scottish runner-up in 2015-16 when he was credited with the SPFL Goal of the Season for a wonder-strike in a 4-0 pulverising of Peterhead.

As a youngster, he worked his way through Farsley Celtic and the youth systems of the Uniteds of Leeds and Newcastle, at one point being goalkeeper for a season with Leeds. A first-team debut came James' way in September 2009 for Newcastle in a League Cup tie with Peterborough United.

Sixteen months later he crossed the Tyne to join Gateshead on loan and later in that calendar year of 2011, had another loan at a higher level with Carlisle United and continued his climb up the loan ladder with further spells with Sheffield Wednesday and MK Dons.

In August 2012, he tasted European football for the first time for Newcastle playing in a UEFA Europa League qualification game and added an English Premier League debut the following month. In 2013, Tavernier had loans to Shrewsbury Town and Rotherham United.

JAMES SCORES FROM THE SPOT IN THE 2-0 EUROPA LEAGUE VICTORY AT STANDARD LIEGE, OCTOBER 2020

He notched his first senior goal on his Millers debut against Gillingham and went on to win promotion with the Yorkshire club, scoring in a penalty shoot-out in the Wembley final against Leyton Orient.

During that summer of 2014, James transferred to Wigan Athletic, but by the next transfer window he was loaned out again, this time to Bristol City before coming to Rangers on 20 July 2015 in a double deal with striker Martyn Waghorn.

Gers fans did not have to wait long to see what Tavernier was capable of. Five days after signing, he marked his debut with a dead-ball goal in a 6-2 Challenge Cup win over Hibs and rapidly went from strength to strength.

Ever since then, James has been a star performer at Ibrox and a major reason Rangers have re-emerged at the peak of the game in Scotland.

WILLIE THORNTON, ONE TIME CUSTODIAN
OF THE RANGERS TROPHY ROOM

THORNTON

Willie Thornton spent his entire career in football, turning to coaching and management after his own playing career came to an end, and both began and ended his career giving service to Rangers.

Born in Winchburg in West Lothian on 3 March 1920,he signed with Rangers as an amateur in March 1936 and was upgraded to the professional ranks the following year. By then he had already made his first-team debut, appearing five times in what would ultimately become Rangers' 1936-37 title winning-season.

Thereafter he became a regular, making 36 appearances in the title-winning season of 1938-39, the last before the outbreak of the Second World War, scoring 23 goals.

Although centre-forwards were supposed to be big and mean, Willie was never even booked during his career. In all, he won four League titles, three Scottish Cups and three League Cups during his time with Rangers, figures that would have been considerably higher had the war not robbed him of some seven years of football. He did, however, win the Military Medal during the conflict for his part in actions in Sicily in 1943.

He retired from playing in 1954 having made 432 appearances for Rangers and scored 255 goals. He then took over as manager of Dundee United, a position he held for five years before replacing Davie Meiklejohn as manager of Partick Thistle. Willie spent nine years with the club before returning to Rangers to become assistant to David White and then Willie Waddell. He died after a brief illness on 26 August 1991.

CARETAKER MANAGER WILLIE THORNTON WITH TRAINER DAVID KINNEAR

TORE ANDRE FLO

GIOVANNI VAN BRONCKHORST

CLAUDIO REYNA

TOP TENS

TOP TEN BIGGEST TRANSFER FEES PAID OUT

Fee	Player	Club
£12.5 million	Tore Andre Flo	Chelsea
£6.5 million	Michael Ball	Everton
£6.5 million	Ryan Kent	Liverpool
£5.8 million	Mikel Arteta	Barcelona
£5.5 million	Andrei Kanchelskis	Fiorentina
£5.0 million	Giovanni Van Bronckhorst	Feyenoord
£4.5 million	Ronald De Boer	Barcelona
£4.5 million	Barry Ferguson	Blackburn Rovers
£4.5 million	Arthur Numan	PSV Eindhoven
£4.3 million	Paul Gascoigne	Lazio

TOP TEN BIGGEST TRANSFER FEES RECEIVED

Fee	Player	Club
£9.0 million	Alan Hutton	Tottenham Hotspur
£8.5 million	Giovanni van Bronckhorst	Arsenal
£8.0 million	Jean-Alain Boumsong	Newcastle United
£7.8 million	Carlos Cuellar	Aston Villa
£7.5 million	Barry Ferguson	Blackburn Rovers
£6.75 million	Tore Andre Flo	Sunderland
£5.6 million	Trevor Steven	Marseille
£5.5 million	Nikica Jelavic	Everton
£4.2 million	Duncan Ferguson	Everton
£4.0 million	Claudio Reyna	Sunderland

UEFA CUP FINAL

Rangers took over Manchester when City's stadium staged the UEFA Cup final against Dick Advocaat's Zenit St. Petersburg who defeated Walter Smith's side 2-0 on 14 May 2008.

The official post-match report to Manchester City council stated that between 150,000 and 160,000 supporters descended on Manchester, declaring it, 'the largest known migration of supporters for a single match.' This was almost four times the 43,878 lucky enough to gain admission to see the big game.

Fiorentina and Sporting Lisbon had been knocked out in the semi and quarter-finals without a goal being conceded, but goals from Igor Denisov and Konstantin Zyryanov left Rangers disappointed, the second goal coming four minutes into added time just as the light blues looked like they might take the final into extra-time.

Jean-Claude Darcheville posed Rangers' main threat with Barry Ferguson hitting the post, but it was future Arsenal man Andrei Arshavin who dictated most of the play and it was the diminutive playmaker who provided the assist for the goal that broke the deadlock after 72 minutes and opened up the defence for the second.

CLAUDIO CANIGGIA CELEBRATES SCORING THE SECOND GOAL AT DUNFERMLINE, 2002-03

UNFORGETTABLE

There was never any doubt that Rangers would win the League title in 1898-99, recording what is still the only 100% record in a major League competition in the world and finishing ten points ahead of their nearest rivals Hearts, with 18 games played and only two points available for a win.

There have been 54 other title wins, some won by a considerable margin, others on the slenderest, but none have ever quite matched the title wins of 2002-03 and 2004-05 for sheer drama.

The 2002-03 season went right down to the wire, with Rangers neck and neck with reigning champions Celtic for virtually the whole of the season. Indeed, so close was the race that after Rangers had lost 2-1 at home to Celtic with just four games to go, the destination of the title was still not guaranteed.

Going into the final game of the season, the two clubs were level on points and goal difference, with Rangers slightly ahead by virtue of having scored more goals than their rivals. This meant that Rangers, away at Dunfermline, had to equal or better whatever Celtic managed at Kilmarnock.

By half time both Glasgow rivals were ahead, Rangers 3-1 up against Dunfermline and Celtic 2-0 in front of Kilmarnock. The second half of both matches was played out with equal drama, Celtic scoring and then missing a penalty whilst Rangers were moving further ahead. A fifth Rangers goal was greeted with the news Celtic had gone 4-0 up - another Celtic goal would give them the title, but as the Rangers match entered virtually the final minute, there was still time for Rangers to get a penalty of their own, which was duly despatched by Mikel Arteta.

The final whistle went at both grounds, Celtic having won 4-0 and Rangers 6-1 to clinch the title for the fiftieth time in their history, by just one goal.

If that was close, then the events of 2004-05 were equally dramatic. Indeed, the events of the final day of the season have entered into folklore as 'Helicopter Sunday'. Going into the final match of the season, Celtic led the table by two points from Rangers and were due to play at Motherwell, where former Rangers legend Terry Butcher was manager.

Rangers meanwhile were the visitors to a Hibernian side that were chasing third spot in the table and with it a place in the UEFA Cup, so they had their own desire to perform well. A goal from Nacho Novo just before the hour mark proved to be the only goal at Easter Road, so thoughts immediately turned to what was happening at Motherwell.

With Chris Sutton having scored for Celtic after just half an hour the omens did not look good, with a young Motherwell side battling hard but getting little or no reward for their efforts.

Then, as the Motherwell and Celtic match headed towards injury time, Scott McDonald scored with an overhead kick. News of this goal was still being cheered at Easter Road when Scott McDonald nipped in to score a second and decisive goal against Celtic with literally the last kick of the game.

Having been chasing the League title all season, Rangers finally got on top in the final minute! So sure were the football authorities that Celtic would win the title, the helicopter carrying the trophy was already on its way to Motherwell for presentation to Celtic, only to have to turn around and head for Edinburgh at the last moment!

NACHO NOVO CELEBRATES SCORING THE ONLY GOAL AT EASTER ROAD, 2004-05

GIOVANNI VAN BRONCKHORST, 1999-2000

BELOW:
VAN BRONCKHORST IN RANGERS LEGENDS ACTION
V AC MILAN GLORIE, MARCH 2012

VAN BRONCKHORST

Born in Rotterdam on 5 February 1975, Giovanni Van Bronckhorst is assured his place in the Rangers record books for being one of the most costly players brought in and the most expensive transfer out again.

He began his career with RKC Waalwijk, but made his name with Feyenoord, joining them in 1994 and spending four years with the Rotterdam club. When Dutch manager Dick Advocaat took over at Ibrox he targeted a number of fellow Dutchmen to join him at the club, paying Feyenoord £5 million to bring Giovanni to Ibrox.

He made his debut in the UEFA Cup tie against Shelbourne and played a significant part in the comeback from 3-0 down to winning 5-3, scoring one of the goals.

Used as an attack minded midfielder, Giovanni would go on to score 22 goals for the club, including 13 in the League, three in the Scottish Cup, one in the League Cup, three in the Champions League and two in the UEFA Cup before a record-breaking £8.5 move to Arsenal in the summer of 2001.

By then he had two League titles, a Scottish Cup and League Cup winners' medals to his name. He struggled to hold down a regular place at Arsenal, prompting a further move to Barcelona in 2003.

A Champions League winner with the Catalan club in 2006, Gio also won two La Liga titles and two Spanish Supercups before completing his club career back at Feyenoord. He saved the best until last, ending his career by captaining the Netherlands in the 2010 FIFA World Cup final, coming off in extra time with the score level before Spain took the trophy.

Moving into management with Feyenoord, van Bronckhorst took the club to their first league title in 18 in 2017 after winning the KNVB Cup a year earlier. In 2020 he spent a year in the lucrative Chinese Super League in charge of Guangzhou R&F.

VAN BRONCKHORST BATTLES WITH OF CELTIC'S PAUL LAMBERT, MARCH 2000

WILLIE WADDELL LEAPS OVER THE CHALLENGE FROM PARTICK THISTLE'S BOBBY GIBB

WADDELL

Willie Waddell's name has become synonymous with the ambitious rebuilding of Ibrox, after the tragic events of 1971, into one of the finest stadiums in the country, but he gave the club exceptional service in a wide variety of other roles.

Born in 1921, Willie had first been associated with Rangers as a player, joining the club in May 1938 and becoming an integral part of the side in the immediate post-war-period when he supplied the crosses for the likes of Willie Thornton that would eventually bring four League titles, two Scottish Cups and three League Cups, having already won a variety of wartime League and cups during the conflict. Willie also won 17 caps for Scotland before his retirement from playing in the summer of 1956, having made 517 appearances for the club.

After a spell in journalism, Willie returned to football as manager of Kilmarnock and set about turning the club's fortunes around. By 1960 he had lifted them into the top reaches of the League finishing runners-up behind Hearts. Kilmarnock were to finish runners-up a further three times in four years, all behind Rangers, before finally lifting the title in 1964-65.

Four years later he was brought back to Rangers to replace David White and the following year delivered the first trophy in six years in the shape of the League Cup.

The Ibrox disaster, together with his own belief that the players would be better working more closely with a younger man on the training field saw Willie Waddell start to take a back seat role.

Whilst he may not have had as much day to day contact with the players, his influence could be seen as Ibrox became transformed.

Although Willie resigned as team manager in 1972 his work was still not done, continuing to serve the club as managing director, general manager and then vice chairman before his death in 1992. Before he died, he saw Ibrox convert itself from an elliptical death trap into a thoroughly modern and impressive stadium, a lasting legacy.

WILLIE WADDELL, LEFT, TALKING TO JOURNALISTS THE DAY AFTER THE IBROX DISASTER

WALLACE

Jock Wallace was the first man to have managed Rangers twice, with both spells in charge ending somewhat unceremoniously. Born in Wallyford on 6 September 1935, Jock signed with Blackpool as an amateur, but was released without ever having played for the first team.

Undeterred Jock went elsewhere and played in goal for Workington Town, Airdrie and West Bromwich Albion as well as a couple of non-League clubs before being appointed player-manager of Berwick Rangers. It was Jock who did most to deny the Rangers strike force in that infamous Scottish Cup tie in 1967, but he did not see that as the pinnacle of his career, working hard to get Berwick challenging for promotion.

Eventually Jock's efforts were rewarded with a move to a bigger club, being appointed assistant manager of Hearts. There the higher profile brought him to the attention of Rangers once again, with Willie Waddell offering Jock the role of coach at Ibrox in June 1970. He worked the players hard, demanding the highest possible levels of fitness and stamina for the challenges ahead and looking to close the gap between them and Celtic.

In 1972 Willie Waddell decided to move into more of an administrative role at the club (he was preoccupied with rebuilding Ibrox into one of the finest stadiums in the country) and Jock was appointed team manager, taking over a side that had just won the European Cup Winners' Cup.

Jock continued Rangers' success, winning the Scottish Cup in 1973 and the League title in 1975, Rangers' first in eleven years. The following year he won every domestic honour, the League, League Cup and Scottish Cup, a treble he was to repeat in 1978.

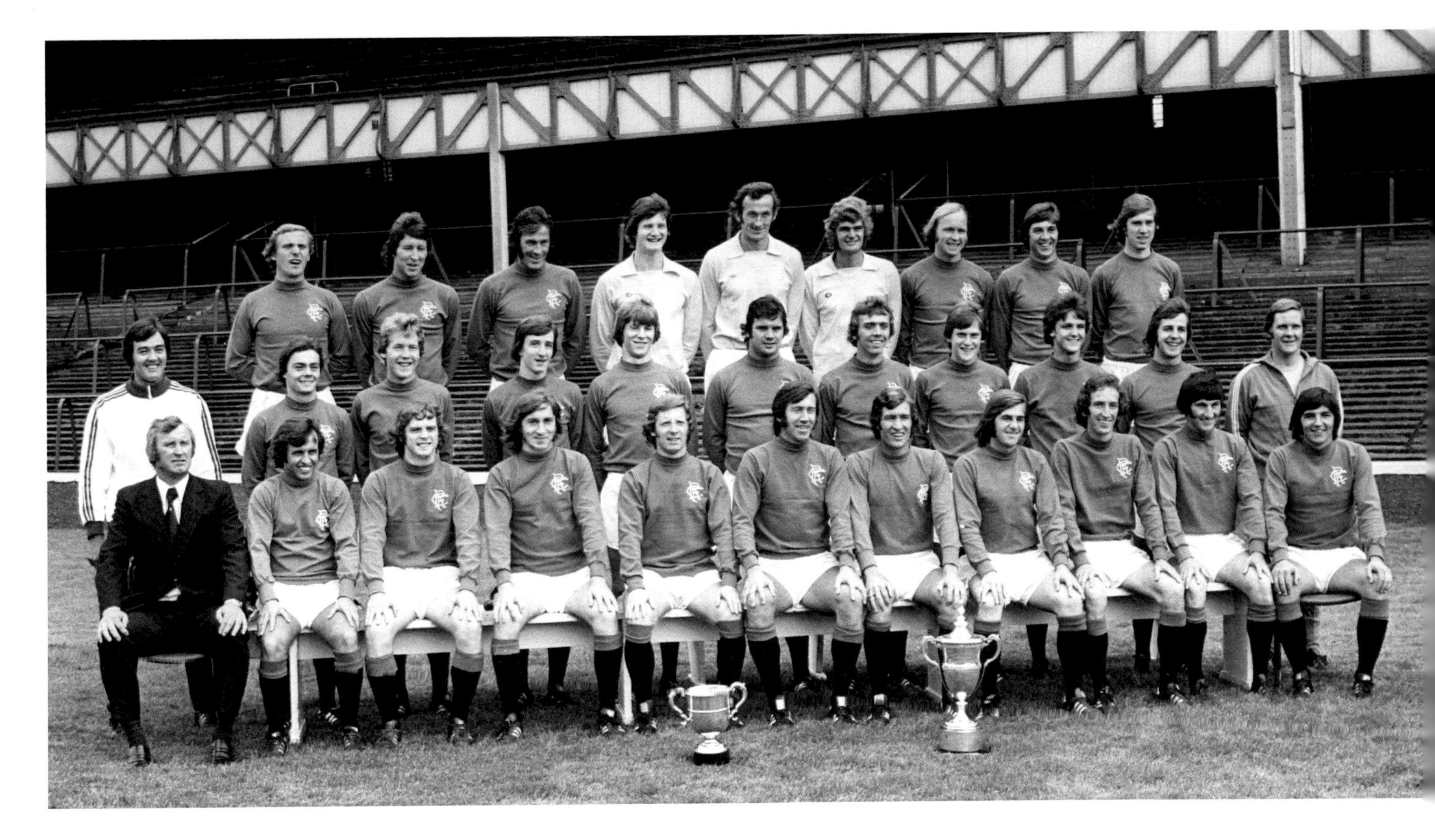

JOCK WALLACE WITH HIS 1975-76 RANGERS SQUAD

Despite this latter success, Jock Wallace resigned soon after, with neither club nor manager revealing the full reasons as to why he had left the club, although it was later claimed that he and Willie Waddell had clashed over player transfers Jock had identified as necessary to the club, but which Waddell wouldn't sanction because it would have diverted funds away from the rebuilding of the stadium.

Jock Wallace went south of the border and took over at Leicester City, taking them into the top flight and the semi-finals of the FA Cup before returning to Scotland to take over at Motherwell in 1982. The following October, following the departure of John Greig (who had replaced Jock Wallace in 1978), Rangers once again turned to Jock Wallace. His second spell in charge brought further success in the shape of consecutive League Cup victories, but it was Rangers' inability to mount a serious title challenge that brought increasing pressure.

The arrival of a new chief executive in the shape of David Holmes, who may already have had Graeme Souness lined up as player-manager, meant Jock's days in charge were numbered and he was sacked in April 1986.
He later went to Spain to manage Seville and was a manager and then director of Colchester United before his death on 24 July 1996 from motor neurone disease.

RAY WILKINS ON ENGLAND DUTY

WILKINS

When Graeme Souness paid Paris St Germain 250,000 for Ray Wilkins in November 1987, there were many who questioned the move for a player already the wrong side of 30 and known for being, at times, an unadventurous player, opting for the safe sideways ball rather than look for a more telling through ball.

Graeme Souness knew what he was buying and in the space of two years Rangers fans came to appreciate what it was Ray brought to the team.

RAY WILKINS IN ACTION V CELTIC, MARCH 1988

Born in Hillingdon on 14 September 1956, Ray had begun his career with Chelsea, being made captain at the age of 18. Later, moves to Manchester United and AC Milan brought him numerous honours and awards, including 84 caps for England, and it was this experience that prompted Graeme Souness to sign him in 1987.

Ray's Ibrox career was to last two years, bringing with it the League title in 1989 and 1990 and the League Cup in 1989 before he moved to London to join QPR.

Wilkins wound down his career with brief spells with Wycombe Wanderers, Hibs, Millwall and Leyton Orient finally totalling a magnificent 848 club games in which he scored 62 times.

He went on to manage QPR and Fulham as well as the national team of Jordan and enjoyed an extensive career as assistant manager with Chelsea, Watford, Millwall, Fulham, Aston Villa and England Under 21s.

Sadly, Wilkins admitted to becoming an alcoholic. He died on 4 April 2018 after a heart attack, at the age of 61. The same day at the Milan derby Franco Baresi laid a bouquet next to a Milan shirt bearing the name Wilkins at the centre spot while the fans displayed a banner translated as, 'Goodbye Ray: Legend of the red and black.'

Ray 'Butch' Wilkins was a legend throughout the game with many Rangers fans judging him to be one of the most skilful midfielders they have had the honour of watching.

WILTON

Officially appointed Rangers' first manager in 1899, William Wilton had joined the club in September 1883, but had never progressed beyond the reserve side as a player. He did, however, possess excellent organisational skills which were to be fully utilised by Rangers, who made him match secretary for the youth and later reserve side, subsequently becoming match secretary for the first team in May 1889.

As a representative of the club he helped organise the Scottish League, serving as treasurer. Whilst he was not responsible for tactics, which was largely left to the players to arrange, his period as match secretary saw the club enjoy considerable success, including two League titles and the Scottish Cup on three occasions. In 1899 the club decided to become a limited company and appointed William to the dual role of secretary-manager, a move that was to see the League title rest at Ibrox on a further seven occasions.

Whilst he was still not responsible for dictating how the club performed on the pitch, he did instigate a series of club rules that remain in force today, including insisting on players being smartly dressed at all times and being reminded from time to time of their responsibilities to the club and its fans.

Rangers had won the League title again in May 1920 when William Wilton set off to spend the Bank Holiday weekend at Gourock. On the first day of his holiday he was relaxing on a friend's yacht when heavy seas threw him overboard and he drowned.

NO.17 CLARE GEMMELL CELEBRATES SCORING V MOTHERWELL, MAY 2021

WOMEN

Rangers Women's FC have been in existence since 2008 when they were initially named Rangers Ladies. The name-change from Ladies to Women came a decade later in 2018.

They came into being having formed a partnership with Paisley Ladies with Drew Todd - a youth academy coach at Ibrox - handed the responsibility of coaching the team who were captained by Scotland international Jayne Sommerville.

Immediately successful with the swift capture of the Scottish Women's First Division, they came close to a first season double, only to lose the Scottish Cup final to Glasgow City.

With Scott Allison having taken over as manager, the Cup final was reached again in 2010. On this occasion, the trophy eluded the Rangers women after losing narrowly to Hibernian.

BRIANNA WESTRUP IN SWPL1 ACTION V CELTIC, APRIL 2021

Four years later runners-up spot in the SWPL represented the club's highest league position to date. Going into the 2021-22 campaign, Women's team boss Malky Thomson was focussing on youth development with centre-back Brianna Westrup appointed captain following the retirement of Clare Gemmell.

As of yet the Women's team have not experienced the level of success associated with the men's team, but it is terrific to see women now an integral part of the club with success surely just a matter of time.

WOODBURN

Willie Woodburn had a 'Never say die' attitude when it came to football, wanting to win every ball in every match and expecting his teammates to do the same. This trait made him extremely popular among the fans, but sometimes upset opponents, match-day officials and even some of his teammates - if Willie thought they weren't pulling their weight, he would let them know in no uncertain terms.

This fiery side of his temperament was to cause him problems during his career, getting sent off four times at a time when even one sending-off was rare and eventually he was handed a sine die suspension from the game in September 1954 for headbutting an opponent in a match against Stirling Albion. He remains the last British footballer to be given a life ban for rough behaviour.

Despite this unfortunate end to his playing career, Willie was an extremely talented centre-half and a member of the 'Iron Curtain' defence, having joined the club as a professional in October 1937 when aged 18. By the time of his enforced retirement he had won four League titles, four Scottish Cups and the League Cup twice, as well as representing Scotland on 24 occasions, proof that he was highly rated. His suspension from the game was lifted in April 1957.

Following his playing days Willie ran a garage before working for the News of the World as a sportswriter and was inducted into the Rangers and Scottish Football Hall of Fame. He passed away on 2 December 2001 at the age of 82.

SCOTLAND'S WILLIE WOODBURN WITH ENGLAND'S TOMMY LAWTON, APRIL 1947

COLIN STEIN HIT THE WINNER AT HIBERNIAN, CHRISTMAS DAY 1971

XMAS DAY

Whilst football matches played on Christmas Day were taken as part and parcel of the festivities in England for many a year, with the last of these being played in 1958, in Scotland these were only played if Christmas Day fell on a Saturday, and then only as part of the normal fixture list.

Thus Christmas Day matches continued in Scotland for some 13 years after they had been halted in England. Here therefore is a list of matches played by Rangers on Christmas Day. With the exception of the 1880 fixture, all of these were League matches, with the fixtures in 1943 and 1945 being wartime League fixtures. The Dumbarton fixture of 1880 was a Scottish Cup quarter-final.

Year	Opponents	Venue	Score
1880	Dumbarton	Home	1-3
1897	Dundee	Home	5-0
1909	Falkirk	Away	1-3
1915	Falkirk	Home	1-0
1920	Clyde	Away	3-1
1926	Dundee United	Away	0-2
1934	Falkirk	Home	1-0
1937	St Johnstone	Away	5-1
1943	Third Lanark	Home	3-1
1945	Clyde	Home	3-1
1947	Dundee	Away	3-1
1948	Falkirk	Away	2-2
1954	Hibernian	Away	1-2
1965	Dunfermline Athletic	Home	2-3
1971	Hibernian	Away	1-0

YOUNG

A big defender, standing some 6' 2" tall and weighing in at 15 stone at his prime, George Young was a colossus for Rangers both on and off the field and an uncompromising and inspirational leader. Born in Grangemouth in 1922, George signed with Rangers as an amateur in 1937 and was upgraded to the professional ranks in 1941.

Whilst centre-half would appear to have been his natural position, the presence of Willie Woodburn in that position meant George was switched to right-back, but together the pair formed part of one of the most successful defences in the domestic game. Not for nothing was it known as the 'Iron Curtain' defence, the foundation upon which Rangers were to win six League titles whilst George was in the side. There were also four Scottish Cup and two League Cup victories to savour, with George scoring twice from the penalty spot in the 1949 Scottish Cup Final against Clyde.

Known as 'Corky' throughout his career on account of the lucky champagne cork he carried around with him, George also won 53 caps for Scotland, captaining the side on 48 occasions, indicative of how highly he was regarded at both club and international level. His playing career came to an end in the summer of 1957 and he went on to manage Third Lanark for three years. He passed away on 10 January 1997.

ZZZ ...MOMENTS TO FORGET

Whilst Rangers' history has, for the most part, been laden with success, there have still been moments that would be better forgotten. Some of these have come in the full gaze of the watching football world, such as the 7 -1 defeat inflicted by Celtic in the League Cup Final in 1957, the very first time the two sides had contested the final.

Whilst Rangers have beaten and lost to Celtic in many cup finals since, neither side has managed to register a victory quite as emphatic as that 7 -1 scoreline, something Rangers would love to repay with interest.

As humiliating as that defeat was, it still does not compare with the events a little under ten years later. By the time January 1967 came around, Rangers were still playing catch up with reigning champions Celtic, having already lost to them in the League Cup Final 1-0 the previous October. On 28 January, thoughts turned to the Scottish FA Cup, with Rangers drawn away to that other Rangers, Berwick.

A record attendance of 13,365 was packed into Shielfield Park, fully expecting Rangers (the Glasgow variety) to rack up a handsome goal tally and progress into the second round.

Things did not go their way, however, for the Berwick goalkeeper performed heroics to keep out everything Rangers threw at him and Sammy Reid popped up at the other end to score the only goal of the game.

It was the first time in 30 years Rangers had gone out of the competition at the first round stage and the first time in the twentieth century they had lost to a team from outside the Scottish top flight. Rangers chairman John Lawrence was so disgusted with the performance he promised that some of the players would never play for the club again, which turned out to be true for two of them.

Meanwhile, national attention was focused on the previously unknown Berwick Rangers players. Whilst Reid may have scored the only goal, the undoubted star performer for Berwick Rangers was goalkeeper Jock Wallace, later to become Rangers manager on two occasions!

Exactly eleven years after the defeat, Rangers were again drawn away to Berwick Rangers in the corresponding round (following re-organisation of the cup for the 1971-72 season, Rangers now entered at the third round); this time Rangers made sure the result went by the form book, winning 4-2.

PREMIER
CHAMPIONS
PREMIERSHIP

SHIP